The Harm of Coercive Schooling

The Harm of Coercive Schooling

PETER GRAY

TIPPING POINTS PRESS
The Alliance for Self-Directed Education
CAMBRIDGE, MA, USA

Published by Tipping Points Press
The Alliance for Self-Directed Education

First paperback edition published in 2020 by Tipping Points Press

ISBN: 978-1-952837-00-5 (paperback)
ISBN: 978-1-952837-01-2 (ebook)

Library of Congress Cataloging-in-Publication Data
Names: Gray, Peter, author.
Title: The Harm of Coercive Schooling
Description: Tipping Points Press, The Alliance for Self-Directed Education [2020] | Includes biographical references and index.
Subjects: Schooling, Psychological child abuse.
Identifiers: ISBN 978-1-952837-00-5 (paperback) | ISBN 978-1-952837-01-2 (ebook)

The chapters published in this book were previously published as separate articles in Peter Gray's column, "Freedom to Learn" in *Psychology Today* and are presented here with permission.

Cover Illustration Credit: Juniper Ingber
Cover & Interior Design Credit: Elliott Beard

Contents

Editor's Preface

Myriad thinkers before our time have diagnosed the ills of conventional educational systems and prescribed their cures. Dr. Peter Gray's magnificent contributions to this vital field, however, transcend the familiar routine of pointing out problems and proposing new methods to replace them. He rightly reframes the issue in the broader terms of civil liberties—in particular, the rights of children—and identifies the primary need for young people to take back their childhood. Peter has spent a remarkable 36-year career researching the relationship children have historically had with play and learning in their societies since the time of hunters and gatherers. In doing so, he has established a broad, humanitarian view of childhood that counteracts our culture's myopic, impersonal focus on assessment and workforce training. This compendium of essays, categorized by subject, catalogues the complete thoughts thus far of Dr. Gray's research on the importance of childhood freedom.

Peter's research and writing have made significant impacts on diverse populations concerned with the wellbeing and education of children, shifting his readers' thinking on children's rights and their understanding of what childhood has looked like over the history of humankind. I have heard innumerable firsthand accounts of the effect of Peter's work on parents, educators, play advocates, young people, and youth rights activists ranging from Sub-Saharan Africa to the Baltic States and from East Asia to South America. For example, a mother in Greece told me how Peter's writing motivated her to withdraw her child from the local school system and start a democratic education movement. A Sudbury school struggling to open in Turkey, where Self-Directed Education is illegal, attested to me that his writing inspired them to try it despite the risk and difficulty. A teenager in the U.S. Midwest attributed Peter's writing as the foundation of her effort to drop out of school and become an unschooler.

This begs the question, what is it about Dr. Gray's insightful research and writing that universally seems to inspire a new generation to risk breaking with convention and to actualize freedom through education, parenting, and personal growth? I cannot speak for all, but I think I may have an inkling. Peter's experience as a research professor of evolutionary, developmental, and educational psychology gives him an advantageous perspective on the subject of child rearing and learning. He is able to draw his readers out of society's normative obsession with assessment and workforce productivity, and compel us to pursue the deeper question of "What is it all for?" He backs up his perspectives with primary research, valid scientific evidence, and detailed explanations of the long history of self-directed childhoods.

In his 2013 book, *Free to Learn: Why Unleashing the Instinct to Play Will Make Our Children Happier, More Self-Reliant, and Better Students for Life*, Dr. Gray grounds his views in rigorous evolutionary research on the universal ways in which indigenous hunters and gatherers raised their young. His analysis shows that children are healthiest and learn most effectively when they are left to playfully explore their natural curiosities in a nurturing environment equipped with the tools of their culture. Dr. Gray observes that for hundreds of thousands of years, constituting nearly all of human history, this was the way in which children were raised. In other words, our species has survived throughout nearly all of our history by being trustful parents, and allowing children to self direct their own childhoods. This realization has given me, and many others, the knowledge and courage to depart and divest from the unnatural, unhealthy, and unjust attitude toward childhood that prevails in most cultures today.

Peter Gray's dedication and contribution to the subject of children's rights has inspired a new generation of advocates, now equipped with his scientific evidence of what is the long-established, just, and healthy way for children to thrive in their development. This compendium of essays, assembled and adapted from his column "Freedom to Learn," appearing in *Psychology Today*, presents the many years of findings and reporting of Dr. Gray's lifelong work. It is a contemporary reader's great fortune to have this compilation available for inspiration and documentation. And it is my great honor to provide you with this work, which also initiates a hopefully long tradition of forthcoming books about the rights of the child. This compendium marks the inaugural publication of Tipping Points Press, dedicated to the advocacy of children's rights, by the Alliance for Self-Directed Education, which Peter Gray helped to found. We look forward to the continuation of pushing forward in advocating for children's rights until we reach that tipping point, when all children are free.

> *Alexander Khost*
> Editor-in-Chief
> Tipping Points Press
> The Alliance for Self-Directed Education
> APRIL 18, 2020

Author's Preface

I have been writing a blog for *Psychology Today* magazine, called "Freedom to Learn," since July, 2008. I have been posting there, at a rate of roughly one per month, articles dealing with child development and education, especially with children's natural ways of educating themselves when they are free to do so.

Over the years I have received many requests, from readers, for bound collections of these articles, arranged by topic, which would make the articles easier to find and easier to give to others than is possible by searching the *Psychology Today* online contents. Now, in collaboration with Tipping Points Press, the new book-publishing arm of the Alliance for Self-Directed Education (ASDE), I am responding to that request.

We are beginning with four collections, published simultaneously. The collection you have in hand is about the harm to children that is perpetrated by our system of compulsory schooling. The other collections in this first set deal, respectively, with the evidence that Self-Directed Education works (that children in charge of their own education educate themselves well); how children acquire academic skills (especially literacy and numeracy) when allowed to do so in their own ways; and the natural, biological drives that underlie children's self-education and the conditions that optimize those drives. The essays have in some cases been modified slightly from the original *Psychology Today* versions, for clarity and to add more recent information.

I thank Rachel Wallach for her excellent, volunteer work in copyediting this collection; Juniper Ingber, who is a young person engaged in Self-Directed Education, for creating the cover illustration; and Alexander Khost, Editor-in-Chief of Tipping Point Press, for making these collections possible. I also thank the editors of *Psychology Today* for their support over the years in my posting these articles.

All profits from the sales of this book and others in the set help support ASDE in its mission to make opportunities for Self-Directed Education available to all families that seek it.

Peter Gray

1

"Why Don't Students Like School?" Well, Duhhhh . . .

Children don't like school because they love freedom

SEPTEMBER 2, 2009

Someone recently referred me to a book they thought I'd like. It's a 2009 book, aimed at teachers of grades K-12, titled *Why Don't Students Like School?* It's by a cognitive scientist and has received rave reviews from countless people involved in the school system. Google the title and author and you'll find many pages of doting reviews and nobody pointing out that the book totally and utterly misses the obvious answer to the question posed by its title.

The book's thesis is that students don't like school because their teachers don't have a full understanding of certain cognitive principles and therefore don't teach as well as they could. They don't present material in ways that appeal best to students' minds. Presumably, if teachers followed the author's advice and used the latest information cognitive science has to offer about how the mind works, students would love school.

Talk about avoiding the elephant in the room!

Any school child brave enough to be honest about it can tell you why students don't like school. School is prison. They may not use those words, because they're too polite, or maybe they've accepted the idea that school is for their own good and therefore it can't be prison. But decipher their words and the translation generally is, "school is prison."

The author of this book surely knows that school is prison. He can't help but know it; everyone knows it. But here he writes a whole book titled *Why Don't Students Like School?*, and not once does he suggest that just possibly they don't like school because they like freedom, and in school they are not free.

I shouldn't be too harsh on this author. He's not the only one avoiding this particular elephant in the room. Everyone who has ever been to school knows that school is prison, but almost nobody says it. It's not polite to say it. We all tiptoe around this truth, that school is prison, because telling the truth makes us all seem so mean. How could all these nice people be sending their children to prison for a good share of the first 18 years of their lives? How could our democratic government, which is founded on principles of freedom and self-determination, make laws requiring children and adolescents to spend a good portion of their days in prison? It's unthinkable, and so we try hard to avoid thinking it. Or, if we think it, we at least don't say it. When we talk about what's wrong with schools we pretend not to see the elephant, and we talk instead about some of the dander that's gathered around the elephant's periphery.

But I think it is time that we say it out loud. School is prison. The only difference I can think of between school and other prisons is that to get into other prison you have to commit a crime, but they put you in school just because of your age. In other respects school is like other prisons. While there you are stripped of your freedom and dignity. You are told exactly what you must do, and you are punished for failing to comply. Actually, in school you must spend more time doing exactly what you are told to do than is true in adult prisons, so in that sense school is worse than other prisons.

At some level of their consciousness, everyone who has ever been to school knows that it is prison. How could they not know? But people rationalize it by saying (not usually in these words) that children need this particular kind of prison and may even like it if the prison is run well. If children don't like school, according to this rationalization, it's not because school is prison, but because the wardens are not kind enough, or amusing enough, or smart enough to keep the children's minds occupied appropriately.

But anyone who knows anything about children and who allows himself or herself to think honestly should be able to see through this rationalization. Children, like all human beings, crave freedom. They hate to have their freedom restricted. To a large extent they use their freedom precisely to educate themselves. They are biologically prepared to do that. Children explore and play, freely, in ways designed to learn about the physical and social world in which they are developing and to acquire the skills needed to navigate that world. In school they are told they must stop following their interests and, instead, do just what the teacher is telling them they must do. That is why they don't like school.

As a society we could, perhaps, rationalize forcing children to go to school if we could prove that they need this particular kind of prison in order to gain the skills and knowledge necessary to become good citizens, to be happy in adulthood, and to get good jobs. Many people, perhaps most people, think this has been proven, because the educational establishment talks about it as if it has. But, in truth, it has not been proven at all.

In fact, for decades, families who have chosen to "unschool" their children, or to send them to schools or learning centers where children are free to follow their own interests, not forced to follow someone else's curriculum, have been proving the opposite. Children who are provided the tools for learning, including access to a wide range of other people from whom to learn, learn what they need to know, and much more, through self-directed playing, exploring, and questioning. There is no evidence at all that children who are sent to prison come out better than those who are provided the tools and allowed to use them freely. How, then, can we continue to rationalize sending children to prison?

I think the educational establishment deliberately avoids looking honestly at the experiences of unschoolers and students at democratic schools, where children are free, because they are afraid of what they will find. If school as prison isn't necessary, then what becomes of this whole huge enterprise, which employs so many and is so fully embedded in the culture?

The book *Why Don't Students Like School?* is in a long tradition of attempts to bring the "latest findings" of psychology to bear on issues of education. None of those attempts have made schools better. All of those efforts have avoided the elephant and focused instead on trying to clean up the dander. But as long as the elephant is there, the dander just keeps piling up.

2

Seven Sins of Our System of Forced Education

Forced education interferes with children's abilities to educate themselves

SEPTEMBER 9, 2009

In my last essay I took a step that, I must admit, made me feel uncomfortable. I said, several times: "school is prison." I felt uncomfortable saying that because school is so much a part of my life and the lives of almost everyone I know. I, like most people I know, went through the full 12 years of public schooling. My mother taught in a public school for several years. My beloved half-sister is a public schoolteacher. I have many dear friends and cousins who are public schoolteachers. How can I say that these good people—who love children and have poured themselves passionately into the task of trying to help children—are involved in a system of imprisoning children? The comments on the essay showed that my references to school as prison made some other people feel uncomfortable also.

Sometimes I find, no matter how uncomfortable it makes me and others feel, I have to speak the truth. We can use all the euphemisms we want, but the literal truth is that schools, as they generally exist in the United States and other modern countries, are prisons. Human beings within a certain age range (most commonly 6 to 16) are required by law to spend a good portion of their time there, and while there they are told what they must do, and the orders are generally enforced. They have no voice in forming the rules they must follow. A prison—according to the common, general definition—is any place of involuntary confinement and restriction of liberty.

Now you might argue that schools as we know them are good, or necessary; but you can't argue that they are not prisons. To argue the latter would be to argue that we do not, in fact, have a system of compulsory education. Either that, or it would be a semantic argument in which you would claim that prison actually means something different from its common, general definition. I think it is important, in any serious discussion, to use words honestly.

Sometimes people use the word prison in a metaphorical sense to refer to any situation in which they must follow rules or do things that are unpleasant. In that spirit, some adults might refer to their workplace as a prison, or even to their marriage as a prison. But that is not a literal use of the term, because those examples involve voluntary, not involuntary, restraint. It is against the law in this and other democratic countries to force someone to work at a job where the person doesn't want to work, or to marry someone that he or she doesn't want to marry. It is not against the law, however, to force a child to go to school; in fact, it is against the law to not force a child to go to school if you are the parent and the child doesn't want to go. (Yes, I know, some parents have the wherewithal to find alternative schooling or provide home schooling that is acceptable to both the child and the state, but that is not the norm in today's society; and the laws in many states and countries work strongly against such alternatives.) So, while jobs and marriages might in some very sad cases feel like prisons, schools generally are prisons.

Now here's another term that I think deserves to be said out loud: forced education. Like the term prison, this term sounds harsh. But, again, if we have compulsory education, then we have forced education. The term compulsory, if it has any meaning at all, means that the person has no choice about it.

The question worth debating is this: Is forced education—and the consequential imprisonment of children—a good thing or a bad thing? Most people seem to believe that it is, all in all, a good thing; but I think that it is, all in all, a bad thing. I outline here some of the reasons why I think this, in a list of what I refer to as "seven sins" of our system of forced education:

1. Denial of Liberty on the Basis of Age

In my system of values, and in that long endorsed by democratic thinkers, it is wrong to deny anyone liberty without just cause. To incarcerate an adult we must prove, in a court of law, that the person has committed a crime or is a serious threat to herself/himself or others. Yet we incarcerate children and teenagers in school just because of their age. This is the most blatant of the sins of forced education.

2. Fostering of Shame, on the One Hand, and Hubris, on the Other

It is not easy to force people to do what they do not want to do. In most schools we no longer use the cane, as schoolmasters once did, but instead rely on a system of incessant testing, grading, and ranking of children to compare them with their peers. We thereby tap into and distort the human emotional systems of shame and pride to motivate children to do the work. Children are made to feel ashamed if they perform worse than their peers and pride if they perform better. Shame leads some to drop out, psychologically, from the educational endeavor and to become class clowns (not too bad), or bullies (bad), or drug abusers and dealers (very bad). Those made to feel excessive pride from the shallow accomplishments that earn them As and honors may become arrogant, disdainful of the common lot who don't do so well on tests; disdainful, therefore, of democratic values and processes (and this may be the worst effect of all).

3. Interference with the Development of Cooperation and Nurturance

We are an intensely social species, designed for cooperation. Children naturally want to help their friends, and even in school they find ways to do so. But our competition-based system of ranking and grading students works against the cooperative drive. Too much help given by one student to another is cheating. Helping others may even hurt the helper, by raising the grading curve and lowering the helper's position on it. Some of those students who most strongly buy into school understand this well; they become ruthless achievers. Moreover, as I have argued elsewhere (see chapters 4 and 5 in this book and chapter 6 in *Mother Nature's Pedagogy*), the forced age segregation that occurs in school itself promotes competition and bullying and inhibits the development of nurturance. Throughout human history, children and adolescents have learned to be caring and helpful through their interactions with younger children. The age-graded school system deprives them of such opportunities.

4. Interference with the Development of Personal Responsibility and Self-Direction

A theme that I develop fully in the fourth book in this series is that children are biologically predisposed to take responsibility for their own education. They play and explore in ways that allow them to learn about the social and physical world around them. They think about their own future and take steps to prepare themselves for it. By confining children to school and to other adult-directed settings, and by filling their time with assignments, we deprive them of the opportunities and time they need to assume such responsibility.

Moreover, the implicit and sometimes explicit message of our forced schooling system is: "If you do what you are told to do in school, everything will work out well for you." Children who buy into that may stop taking responsibility for their own education. They may assume falsely that someone else has figured out what they need to know to become successful adults, so they don't have to think about it. If their life doesn't work out so well, they take the attitude of a victim: "My school (or parents or society) failed me, and that's why my life is all screwed up."

5. Linking of Learning with Fear, Loathing, and Drudgery

For many students, school generates intense anxiety associated with learning. Students who are just learning to read and are a little slower than the rest feel anxious about reading in front of others. Tests generate anxiety in almost everyone who takes them seriously. Threats of failure and the shame associated with failure generate enormous anxiety in some. I have found in my college teaching of statistics that a high percentage of students, even at my rather elite university, suffer from math anxiety, apparently because of the humiliation they have experienced pertaining to math in school. A fundamental psychological principle is that anxiety inhibits learning. Learning occurs best in a playful state, and anxiety inhibits playfulness. The forced nature of schooling turns learning into work. Teachers even call it work: "You must do your work before you can play." So learning, which children biologically crave, becomes toil—something to be avoided whenever possible.

6. Inhibition of Critical Thinking

Presumably, one of the great general goals of education is the promotion of critical thinking. But despite the lip service that educators devote to that goal, most students—including most "honors students"—learn to avoid thinking critically about their schoolwork. They learn that their job in school is to get high marks on tests and that critical thinking only wastes time and interferes. To get a good grade, you need to figure out what the teacher wants you to say and then say it. I've heard that sentiment expressed countless times by college students as well as by high-school students, in discussions held outside the classroom. I've devoted a lot of effort toward promoting critical thinking at the college level; I've developed a system of teaching designed to promote it, written articles about it, and given many talks about it at conferences on teaching. But, truth be told, the grading system, which is the chief motivator in our system of education, is a powerful force against honest debate and critical thinking in the classroom. In a system in which we teachers do the grading, few students are going to criticize or even question the ideas we offer; and if we try to induce criticism by grading for it, we generate false criticism.

7. Reduction in Diversity of Skills, Knowledge, and Ways of Thinking

By forcing all schoolchildren through the same standard curriculum, we reduce their opportunities to follow alternative pathways. The school curriculum represents a tiny subset of the skills and knowledge that are important to our society. In this day and age, nobody can learn more than a sliver of all there is to know. Why force everyone to learn the same sliver? When children are free— as I have observed at the Sudbury Valley School and others have observed with unschoolers— they take new, diverse, and unpredicted paths. They develop passionate interests, work diligently to become experts in the realms that fascinate them, and then find ways of making a living by pursuing their interests. Students forced through the standard curriculum have much less time to pursue their own interests, and many learn well the lesson that their own interests don't really count; what counts is what's measured on the schools' tests. Some get over that, but too many do not.

This list of "sins" is not novel. Many teachers I have spoken with are quite aware of all of these detrimental effects of forced education, and many work hard to try to counteract them. Some try to instill as much of a sense of freedom and play as the system permits; many do what they can to mute the shame of failure and reduce anxiety; most try to allow and promote cooperation and compassion among the students, despite the barriers against it; many do what they can to allow and promote critical thinking. But the system works against them. It may even be fair to say that teachers in our school system are barely freer to teach as they wish than students are to learn as they wish. (But teachers, unlike students, are free to quit; so they are not in prison.)

I must also add that human beings, especially young ones, are remarkably adaptive and resourceful. Many students find ways to overcome the negative feelings that forced schooling engenders and to focus on the positive. They fight the sins. They find ways to cooperate, to play, to help one another overcome feelings of shame, to put undue pride in its place, to combat bullies, to think critically, and to spend some time on their true interests despite the forces working against them in school. But to do all this while also satisfying the demands of forced education takes great effort, and many do not succeed. At minimum, the time and energy students must spend on wasteful busywork and just following orders in school detracts greatly from the time and energy they can use to educate themselves.

I have listed here "seven sins" of forced education, but I have resisted the temptation to call them the seven sins. There are no doubt more than seven and you can probably list some more yourself.

Finally, I add that I do not believe that we should just do away with schools and replace them with nothing. Children educate themselves, but we adults have a responsibility to provide settings that allow them to do that in an optimal manner.

3

Schools Are Good for Showing Off, Not for Learning

Here's one explanation of the education gap, and why it keeps increasing

SEPTEMBER 19, 2013

Suppose you are a student in a typical high school course and a magic fairy offers you the following choice: (1) You will learn the material in the course well, but will get a low grade (a D); or (2) you will not learn the material, but will get a high grade (an A). Which would you choose? Be honest.

Nearly all students (except for a few rebels) would unhesitatingly choose the second alternative. Students are rational beings. They know that school is about grades, not learning. If they ever need to know the material they can always learn it on their own, in a far more efficient way than they can at school. On the other hand, they can never erase that awful D. It would be stupid to choose the first alternative. By the time they have reached high school, all students know that.

Schools are for showing off, not for learning. When we enroll our children in school, we enroll them into a never-ending series of contests—to see who is best, who can get the highest grades or the highest scores on standardized tests, who can win the most honors, who can make it into the most advanced placement classes, who can get into the best colleges. We see those grades and hoops jumped through as measures not only of our children, but also of ourselves as parents. We find ways, subtly or not so subtly, to brag about them to our friends and relatives. All this has nothing to do with learning, and, really, we all know it. We rarely even bother to think about what our children are actually learning in school; we only care about the grades. We, the parents, maybe even more than our kids, think it would be stupid for our kids to choose the first alternative over the second. We would forbid them from making that choice, if we could.

If schools were for learning rather than showing off, we would design them entirely differently. They would be places where people could follow their own interests, learn what they want to learn, try out various career paths, make plans for the future, and prepare themselves for that future. Everyone would be doing different things, at different times, so there would be no basis for comparison. People would learn to read when they feel a desire or need to learn to read, and we would help them do it if they wanted help. The focus would be on cooperation, not competition. That's what occurs at certain democratic schools, which are for learning, not for showing off, and such schools have proven remarkably effective.

One thing we know about learning is that it is inhibited by the kinds of pressures that we use at schools to motivate performance. Many psychological experiments have shown that contests and evaluations of all sorts lead those who already know well how to perform a task to do it even better than they otherwise would, but has the opposite effect on people who don't know it so well. For example, in one research study conducted many years ago, psychologists observed people playing friendly games of eight-ball at the university's pool hall (Michaels et al., 1982). At first they watched from a distance, so the players wouldn't know they were being observed, and then they moved in close and observed deliberately, making it obvious that they were evaluating performance. The result was that those who were already good, when not observed closely, performed even better when they knew they were being evaluated; but those who were just beginners, learning how to play, performed worse when evaluated. The same has been found for many kinds of tasks—intellectual as well as athletic or manual. Showing off is facilitated by evaluation and contests, but such pressures inhibit learning. And yet, in our constant attempts (supposedly) to increase learning at school, we keep raising the pressure, and then wonder why it doesn't work.

Much has been written about the education gap between children from economically richer and poorer families in the United States. It's interesting to note that over the same period of time that pressures to perform well in school have been increasing, that gap has grown ever larger. In fact, one study (Reardon, 2012) showed that the gap in standardized test scores between the affluent and non-affluent grew by about 40 percent between the 1960s and about 2010.

I'm sure that lots of factors figure into this education gap, but here's one I'd like you to consider. Let's suppose that children from economically better off families learn, at home, much of what they are tested on in school. They perform well under the pressure of tests and the constant evaluation that occurs at school, because they already know a lot of what is being taught. They are used to this way of thinking. Let's suppose that children from economically worse off families don't learn so much, at home, of what they are tested on in school. They perform poorly on the tests, because they don't already know it. The high pressure of constant testing and evaluation, coupled with the embarrassment and shame of failure, makes it very difficult for them to learn at school what the others had already learned at home.

The failure may lead them to accept, fatalistically, a belief in their own stupidity, which may cause them to drop out of the whole process, mentally if not physically. In other words, I suggest, the high-pressure environment drives a wedge between those who already know and those who don't already know, causing the gap to increase from year to year in school. And, as the pressure to perform well increases, the wedge widens.

If we really want to reduce the education gap, we must design schools for learning, not for showing off.

References

Michaels, J. W., Blommel, J. M., Brocato, R. M., Linkous, R. A., & Rowe, J. S. (1982). Social facilitation and inhibition in a natural setting. *Replications in Social Psychology*, 2, 21–24.

Reardon, S. F. (2012). The widening academic achievement gap between the rich and the poor. *Community Investments*, 24 (2), 19-39.

4

School Bullying

A Tragic Cost of Undemocratic Schools

*Anti-bullying laws will work only
when students make the laws*

MAY 12, 2010

Let's say you are 15 years old, or 13, or 11, and for some reason—a reason over which you have no control—you have
been singled out by your schoolmates as an object for scorn
and humiliation. Every day at school, for you, is another
day in hell. You are called "whore," "bitch," "slut;" or "fag,"
"pussy," "scum;" or worse. People deliberately bump into
you and knock your books out of your hands in the hallway.
Nobody sits with you at lunch, or, if they do, those people are
harassed until they stop sitting with you. These bullies are not
the brutish looking comic-strip bullies whom nobody likes
and who steal kids' lunch money. No, these bullies are among
the popular kids—the athletes, cheerleaders, preppies. They
are popular not just with most of the other kids but also with

the teachers, school administrators, and adults in the larger community.

The law requires that you attend school, regardless of how you feel about it and how you are treated. You are not one of the privileged group whose parents have the means to send them to a private alternative school or to convince the school board that they can educate them adequately at home. You have no choice.

What do you do? If you are like most of the hundreds of thousands of picked-on kids who suffer like this every day, you somehow suck it up. You harden yourself and somehow survive it. You may be the only person who will ever know the full extent of your suffering. You may think about killing yourself; you may even fantasize some violent revenge against the whole school, as the whole school seems to be your enemy. If you are like most kids, such thoughts remain in the realm of fantasy. But every once in a while, in a particularly vulnerable person, the despair or rage or both erupt into violence, either against the self or against the whole school, and only then does school bullying become an issue to the larger community.

Here's how Helen Smith, in her book *The Scarred Heart*, tells one such story, that of the suicide of 13-year-old April Michelle Himes of Richland, Washington:

> Kids at school called her fat, threw things at her and pushed her around. They ridiculed her with rumors that she stuffed tissues in her bra. She attempted suicide and her parents admitted her to an inpatient mental hospital

program and sought counseling but said it didn't help. After missing fifty-three out of the required one hundred and eighty days of school, she was told that she would have to return to school or appear before a truancy board which could then send her to a juvenile detention center. She decided the better alternative was to go into her bedroom and hang herself with a belt. . . . In times past, she could have just dropped out of school, but now kids like her are trapped by compulsory education.

In my home state of Massachusetts we've been hearing a lot recently about school bullying and suicide. A year ago (from the time of this writing), headlines were made when 11-year-old Charles Joseph Walker-Hoover hanged himself rather than face another day of bullying at the supposedly "good" charter school he attended in Springfield. Then, in January of this year, Phoebe Prince, a 15-year-old immigrant from Ireland, hanged herself after months of bullying by students at the public school she attended in the affluent community of South Hadley.

The outrage that followed Prince's suicide, coming so soon after Walker-Hoover's, forced the hands of the Massachusetts legislature. Just last week they passed, unanimously, an antibullying bill that was then immediately signed into law by the governor. The whole state felt that something had to be done, so that Charles's and Phoebe's deaths would not have been in vain. So they created a law.

I'm not surprised by the legislators' unanimous votes for this bill, nor by the governor's well-publicized signing of it.

Given the emotional climate, they probably saw no other choice. Anyone who voted against it would have been seen as unsympathetic to the grieving parents and soft on bullying. But this new law is not going to solve the bullying problem, and it will almost certainly create legal and bureaucratic nightmares.

Why Anti-Bullying Legislation Will Not Solve the Bullying Problem

The new anti-bullying law requires that every school employee—including cafeteria workers, janitors, and bus drivers as well as teachers and administrators—report any bullying incident that they see to the principal, who is then required to investigate the incident and take appropriate disciplinary action. In addition, the law requires that every student in Massachusetts, from kindergarten through 12th grade, in every school, participate every year in an "anti-bullying curriculum." On the surface, these may look like good things, but you don't have to scratch very deeply to see the problems.

The first problem with the reporting requirement is that very often—maybe most often—the staff member will have no way to know whether a particular act represents good-natured teasing or real bullying. This is especially true in large schools, where individual staff members don't know everyone. Teasing among friends is a normal, healthy part of adolescence, especially for boys. The best of friends may repeatedly call one another names that sound horrid to outsiders. For many boys, this is their way of hugging.

A cafeteria worker hears a kid calling another kid "loser" a couple of times and then, by law, has to report it and the principal has to investigate it. This is going to keep the principal very busy and will cause a lot of perfectly good, normal, compassionate kids to get into trouble. It'll be like the no-tolerance policy on weapons, which has led kids to get suspended for such infractions as bringing a nail clipper to school; or like the no-tolerance policy on sexual harassment, which caused a third-grade boy to be suspended for kissing a little girl on the cheek. Civil liberties lawyers in Massachusetts are already saying that the new law is likely to run afoul of free speech rights. It will be one more form of top-down control over the behavior of kids in school; one more requirement that makes school feel even more restrictive and prison-like than it already does.

Another problem with the reporting requirement is that it will lead the bullies to hide their bullying from adults even more effectively than they already do. The modern-day bullies that have driven kids to suicide are, by all reports, already very good at hiding their transgressions and looking innocent to adults. This is why teachers and principals so often fail to believe the victims, or the victims' parents, when they are told about harassment. They don't see it. In their view the accused are among the best kids in the school, so they jump to the conclusion that the complaint must represent a psychological problem on the part of the complainer, and then they recommend therapy. The new law is not going to solve this problem. It's still going to be one kid's word against the words of a whole group of other kids; and the latter will often be the smoother talkers.

A third problem with the reporting requirement is that it will cause the "us versus them" gulf between students and staff at schools to become even wider than it was before. Kids will feel that they have to behave even more differently when a staff member is around than is already the case. Because staff members must bring them up for even minor infractions of the new speech code, staff will appear more than ever to be the enemy. So, students' reports to teachers and principals about harassment will be seen as tattling to the enemy, even more than it already is; and students who have the gall to make such reports will be singled out for further abuse, even more than they already are.

What about the other part of the law, the part that requires students to participate every year in an anti-bullying curriculum? A new course, a new curriculum, a new set of tests—these have become the knee-jerk reactions of our culture to every problem that we perceive among kids. In fact, many anti-bullying school programs and courses have been tried over the past 20 years, in other countries as well as in the United States, and many outcome studies have been conducted to see if they work. So far, no program has proven itself to be very effective.

Two major reviews of such outcome research have been published, and both concluded that there is little if any evidence that any of the programs tried so far produce meaningful positive gains (Merrell et al., 2008; Smith et al., 2004). At best, such programs may produce slight decreases in bullying, and at worst they may produce slight increases in bullying. The same has been found for top-down programs aimed at modifying other aspects of adolescents' behavior. For example, the much-touted D.A.R.E. program designed to make kids immune to the temptations of drugs has been shown time and again to be ineffective, and a few years ago it was included, in an article published by the American Psychological Society, in a list of interventions that are more likely to cause harm than good (Lilienfeld, 2007).

The Root Cause of School Bullying

Bullying occurs regularly when people who have no political power and are ruled in top-down fashion by others are required, by law or economic necessity, to remain in that setting. It occurs regularly, for example, in prisons. Those who are bullied can't escape, and they have no legislative or judicial power to confront the bullies. They may report bullying to the prison guards and warden, but the guards and warden may not know whom to believe and may have greater vested interest in hiding bullying than in publicizing it and dealing with it openly.

Recently I read the acclaimed book by Chen Guidi and Wu Chuntau, Will the Boat Sink the Water?, about peasant life in modern day China. The peasants are not allowed to move off the land and they are governed, top down, by petty bureaucrats. The peasants have no political power and no due process of law, and so the bullies, who can best intimidate others, rise to the top.

Should we be surprised to discover that at least some of our schoolchildren respond to forced confinement and dictatorial governance in the same manner as prisoners and Chinese peasants?

In our culture's fondest image of schools, the teachers and principals are infinitely kind, nurturing, and wise adults who know what's best for kids and can solve their problems. But really, of course, teachers and principals are human beings, with all the foibles of human beings everywhere. Most are indeed kind people, but they are far from all knowing or all wise; and nobody, truly nobody, is above self-interest. As a nation we decided long ago that there is no such thing as a benign dictatorship. To have a moral society the people who are governed must do the governing. That's our foundational principle as a nation, and if our children are to be educated for democracy, wouldn't it be nice if our schools, where children spend so much of their lives, were living embodiments of democracy?

There is only one way to get rid of the bullying and the general sense of unfairness that pervades our schools, and that is to restructure radically the way the schools are governed. If our children are required to be in school, then they must be granted a real voice in the way the school is run. If they are not granted such a voice, then school is prison and we can expect students to react in many of the same ways that prisoners everywhere react.

I've been involved for many years with a school where the students and staff together, on a one-person-one-vote basis, make all of the school rules and where the rules are enforced through a judicial system in which students of all ages serve as jurors. This school, like any other, has students who are potential bullies (for who is not potentially a bully?), but its democratic governance is remarkably effective at nipping incipient bullying before it becomes hurtful.

Because the students have power, they feel ownership of the school and have a vested interest in keeping it peaceful. Their legal power promotes an attitude of responsibility, which leads them to use not just the school's legislative and judicial systems but also the full force of peer pressure and friendly persuasion to promote peace and justice. There is no "us versus them" distinction between staff and students at this school. They work together to create a community in which people can feel free and unafraid. I'll say more about all this in the next essay, where I'll present a tried and true formula for creating a school that truly is a moral community.

References

Lilienfeld, S. O. (2007). Psychological treatments that cause harm. Perspectives on *Psychological Science*, 2, 53-70.

Merrell, K. W., et al. (2008). How effective are school bullying intervention programs? A meta-analysis of intervention research. *School Psychology Quarterly*, 23, 26-42.

Smith, J. D., et al. (2004). The effectiveness of whole-school antibullying programs: A synthesis of evaluation research. *School Psychology Review*, 33, 547-560.

5

Freedom from Bullying

How a School Can Be a Moral Community

*Every school should be, first and foremost,
a caring, safe, moral community*

JUNE 8, 2010

Many years ago, as part of my early studies of the Sudbury Valley School, I sat in on a school meeting at which the main agenda item had to do with a complaint made about a new student's clothing. A new teenaged enrollee had been coming to school wearing a leather jacket with a swastika painted on it. At most schools this kind of offence would be quickly and efficiently handled by the principal, who would call the student into his or her office and order the student to remove the jacket and never bring it back to school. But that's not how Sudbury Valley handles things. Sudbury Valley, the pioneering democratic school located in Framingham, Massachusetts, has no principal. It is run, entirely run, in democratic fashion by the School Meeting, which includes all students (age 4 on through high-school age) and staff members together.

The debate that I listened to that day was one befitting the Supreme Court of the United States. There was talk on the one hand of freedom of speech. Did freedom of speech include the right to wear a swastika? I remember one teenaged girl thoughtfully raising the question this way: "Suppose we ban the swastika? Does that mean we could also ban the hammer and sickle, under which terrible atrocities were committed? And what, then, about the American flag? Some people might be offended by it, because of atrocities such as slavery and the mass murder of Native Americans that were committed under this banner. Once we start interfering with free speech, where do we stop?"

On the other side, several presented the argument that the swastika is a hate symbol in a way that the hammer and sickle or the flag of any other country is not. In this discussion, history was presented, not to teach history, but simply as part of the process of putting forth an argument that was directly germane to the decision that the group had to make. As the debate continued, the tension between the right of free speech and the right to freedom from offensive speech came into sharp focus.

Most of the people who spoke were staff members and older students, but many younger students were present, by choice, as nobody is required to attend school meetings. I could see by their expressions that even the youngest were fully engaged by the discussion. When it came time to vote, their vote was truly informed. They had heard all the arguments, on both sides of the question. An issue about clothing had become a deeply moral question about freedom and how one person's freedom sometimes conflicts with another person's freedom, which is why laws are needed. For the record, the swastika was banned, and the school now has a general rule against the display of hate symbols and the use of words that are commonly understood as expressions of hate toward any group of people, even where hate was not intended.

What does this have to do with bullying? Everything.

In the standard school, the principal, in demanding that the student not wear the swastika, would himself have been engaged in an act of bullying. He would have been using his superior power to inflict his will upon the student, who had no power in that setting. The only lesson that the swastika-wearing student would likely have taken away is that "might makes right"—the lesson of a bullying environment.

At Sudbury Valley, the entire community of people who were affected by the decision made the decision. It was made thoughtfully, morally, through established democratic procedures. The swastika-wearing student, who had the same right to vote as everyone else, knew that it wasn't just one person but the majority of people—including his age-mates as well as the adults and little kids—who were opposed to his wearing that jacket. And he could hear the reasons, presented not by some superior, but developed in an open discussion in which all voices were heard. At the same time, those who were offended by the swastika, and who felt bullied by the student's wearing of it, learned that they didn't have to accept such bullying. They could voice their concern, and their voice was heard and taken seriously by the whole community. That is the messy, inefficient system called democracy.

Some years later, my graduate student Jay Feldman spent hundreds of hours at Sudbury Valley, observing and making notes on students' interactions, both indoors and outdoors on the school campus. His main goal was to understand how education occurs in the school's free environment, but in his report he also noted the astonishing lack of any persistent bullying at the school. Many of the vignettes that he recorded demonstrate ways by which the students themselves, in this environment, nip bullying in the bud when it begins to occur (for examples, see Gray & Feldman, 2004).

Feldman's observations made clear that one potent force against bullying at the school derives from the free age mixing that occurs there. The presence of little children, who are known to all, seems to bring out the nurturing qualities in older children, and the spirit of nurturance then transfers even to interactions among age-mates. Another potent force, however, clearly comes from the democratic procedures through which the school operates and the spirit of equality and respect for one another that such procedures engender. That is my focus here.

One of the school's most frequently cited rules—made, of course, through democratic vote of the School Meeting—is that referred to as Infringement of Rights. Basically, the rule is this: If you say or do something to someone that is potentially offensive to that person, and if that person asks you to stop but you don't stop, then you have infringed upon that person's right not to be harassed, and that person, or anyone else, can then "bring you up" to the Judicial Committee. The Judicial Committee, or JC, is a standing jury, which meets every day.

It is composed of school members of all ages—there is always at least one little kid, one middle kid, two older kids, and one staff member—who serve for a certain designated period of time.

Most often, in cases of unwanted teasing, for example, the JC attempts to mediate the case; that is, to bring it to a conclusion satisfactory to both parties without any formal charges. The accused may apologize and the accuser may accept the apology after explaining how the teasing made him or her feel, and that may be the end of it. If such teasing were to occur again, however, the JC would have to decide on some appropriate consequence for the person who inflicted the teasing. Perhaps that person would be banned, for a week, from being anywhere near the person he or she had been harassing.

What a simple, elegant rule! It solves the problem (in most cases) of deciding whether or not a specific name, joke, or action is "all in good fun" or harassment. It's harassment if the target says, seriously, "I don't like this, so please stop it." In some cases, however, it takes students a while to learn that they have the right to voice objections to teasing, and in those cases someone else may bring up the offender if he or she believes that the target felt harassed or might reasonably have felt so. When this happens, the arguments before the JC become more complicated. Not surprisingly, most complaints about teasing are brought by little kids against other little kids. Older kids, in this environment, have usually learned to settle such disputes and respect one another's rights without the JC.

Serving on the JC, which everyone does from time to

time, is itself an education in concern for others. On the JC, students of all ages have the mature task of listening to and trying to understand both parties in a dispute. The school's judicial system is not designed for education—it is designed for the very practical purpose of settling disputes—but, in fact, each case tried is a real-life lesson in human sensitivity for everyone concerned.

Sudbury Valley calls itself a school, but it is first and foremost a democratic, moral community. Every school member, regardless of age and regardless of status as student or staff, has legal power equivalent to every other member of the school. The official system of authority at the school is not one of bullying; it is not top-down authority based on power differentials. Every voice is heard, and when people are listened to and respected they no longer have a need to bully. In fact, in that environment, people learn that bullying backfires. It does not achieve any useful ends, and it puts you at odds with people you respect, and who respect you, in ways that make you uncomfortable but not rejected and lead you to change your ways. Wouldn't it be nice if every school were a democratic, moral community?

Reference

Gray, P. and Feldman, J. (2004). Playing in the Zone of Proximal Development: Qualities of Self-Directed Age Mixing Between Adolescents and Young Children at a Democratic School. *American Journal of Education*, 110, 108-145.

6

Cheating in Science

School is a Breeding Ground

Cheating is most frequent among the "best" students today

OCTOBER 5 AND 30, 2010

(This essay was originally published in two installments.)

I begin with a true and tragic story. Many years ago I was a graduate student conducting research in one of the top biopsychology laboratories in the country. The lab chief was one of a handful of the world's most prominent research psychologists at that time, and many in the lab believed he was headed for a Nobel Prize.

As is often the case, this lab head was not doing hands-on research himself. He was busy writing articles and grant proposals and traveling around giving speeches. A fleet of graduate students and postdoctoral fellows conducted the research. He would put his name on reports of research that he had helped to design but that others had conducted. He didn't even understand fully the equipment that was used in those experiments.

A certain postdoctoral fellow in the lab—I'll call him Henry—was getting most of the fabulous results. At about the same time that I received my PhD and took an assistant professorship at a more humble institution, Henry accepted an offer to become full professor at one of the most prestigious psychology departments in the country. The task of continuing the line of research he had been doing was then turned over to an excellent, conscientious graduate student in the lab he had left. That graduate student could not replicate any of Henry's famous findings. This led to repeated calls to Henry to come back and demonstrate how he got those fabulous results, to which there was no satisfactory response. With continued failures to replicate, and with continued defensiveness and evasiveness on the part of Henry, the suspicion grew, usually unstated, that Henry may have made up those findings. And then the tragedy happened. Henry committed suicide.

What a shock that was to me. I can't say that I really liked Henry; his ambition was such that he rubbed those who were beneath him, including me, the wrong way. But I knew him and felt I understood him. He was a real flesh and blood person to me, and when I heard of his suicide I cried. I could see him as a frail person—despite his burly physique and blustering style—caught up in a drive toward self-advancement, in a lab that was rewarding the "right" findings and had little interest in the "wrong" ones. He was not, in truth, a scientist at all. He wasn't interested in the questions he was supposedly pursuing in the lab. When the foundation for his self-advancement was pulled out from under him he toppled; he could no longer see any purpose in living.

The Frequency of Cheating in Science

I've been thinking lately about the whole question of cheating in science. It has been brought to mind, in part, by recent media coverage of a new exposed case of fabricating data by a celebrated research psychologist at Harvard University. How common is scientific fraud? Nobody really knows. Defenders of science's purity often argue that such fraud is very rare, the product of a tiny number of "bad apples." But I doubt that. My suspicion is that the cases of fraud that are exposed are just the tip of the iceberg.

I've heard people argue that it would be against anyone's self-interest to cheat in science because cheating will be caught when someone tries to replicate the experiment and fails. But, in truth, replication is rare in most areas of science. Most scientists want to do something new, and funding agencies rarely provide grants to repeat already published experiments. Even when replications are conducted and fail, there are almost always ways to explain the discrepancies without suggesting fraud. No experiment can possibly be an exact replication of a previous one. This is especially true in the behavioral sciences. The subjects are different (different people, or rats, or ant colonies), the time in history is different, the ambient conditions (temperature, barometric pressure, color of the walls) are different, and so on. Failure to replicate may well be taken to indicate that the original findings are not as "robust" as previously believed, but it is almost never taken as evidence of fraud.

Even in the case of Henry, where every attempt was made to keep conditions exactly the same as those in the original experiments, the researchers continued to "explain" the failure, at least publicly, in terms of hypothetical changed conditions. They suggested in one article, for example, that the company from which they obtained the rats may have been breeding the animals in a way that had altered their behavioral reactions. My guess is that if Henry had remained alive and had been formally accused of fraud, nobody would have been able to prove it.

Proof of fraud in science rarely if ever comes from failure to replicate. It comes, most often, when the perpetrator of the fraud becomes so brazen that he or she fabricates or alters data in ways that make the fraud obvious to others. The cheating at Harvard was caught, apparently, because the cheater began to pressure his graduate students to get the results he wanted, which led them to become whistleblowers, which, in turn, led to an investigation revealing that his recorded data did not match that in his published papers (Wade, 2010).

Some other scientists have been caught cheating because their fabricated data, quite literally, was too good to be true. There is always a certain degree of random variability in real data, and repeated data sets that have no or almost no variability are powerful evidence of fabrication. You have to be either very brazen or very stupid to get caught at cheating in science.

Over the years a number of surveys have been conducted in which scientists were asked to report, on an anonymous questionnaire, on their own fraudulent behavior. A recent meta-analysis of those surveys revealed that, on average, about two percent of scientists admitted to fabricating or falsifying data, and 14 percent said that they had personal evidence of such behavior in one or more of their colleagues (Fanelli, 2009). The percentage admitting to fraud was highest among scientists doing pharmaceutical, clinical, and other medical research, which either means that researchers in those fields fabricate lab data more often or lie less often on questionnaires than do researchers in other fields.

As the author of the meta-analysis pointed out, the two-percent figure is the lowest possible estimate of the percentage of scientists who have deliberately falsified data. No respondents would say that they had behaved fraudulently if they hadn't, but many, even on an anonymous questionnaire, might be expected to lie in the opposite direction. The meta-analysis also revealed that a full third of the respondents to the surveys admitted to more subtle forms of scientific cheating, such as failing to report data that contradicted their theories or dropping data points from analyses because of a "gut feeling" that they were inaccurate.

The purpose of science is to discover truths. Cheating completely defeats the purpose. Why, then, do scientists cheat? I think part of the answer is this: Many so-called scientists are not, in their heads, really scientists. Instead, they are still students, going through one hoop after another to reach the next level. To them, cheating in science is like cheating in school, and "who doesn't do that?" Let me elaborate on that suggestion.

The Structure of Compulsory Schooling Promotes Cheating

Our system of compulsory (forced) schooling is almost perfectly designed to promote cheating. That is even truer today than in times past. Students are required to spend way more time than they wish doing work that they did not choose, that bores them, that seems purposeless to them. They are constantly told about the value of high grades. Grades are used as essentially the sole motivator. Everything is done for grades. Advancement through the system, and eventual freedom from it, depends upon grades.

Students become convinced that high grades and advancement to the next level are the be-all and end-all of their schoolwork. By the time they are 12 or 13 years old, most are realistically cynical about the idea that school is fundamentally a place for learning. They realize that much of what they are required to do is senseless and that they will forget most of what they are tested on shortly after the test. They see little direct connection—because there usually is none—between their school assignments and the real world in which they live. They learn that their own questions and interests don't count. What counts are their abilities to provide the "correct" answers to questions that they did not ask and that do not interest them. And "correct" means the answers that the teachers or the test-producers are looking for, not answers that the students really understand to be correct.

A high-school student whom I was once trying to help with math homework summed it up nicely to me. After a few minutes of pretending politely to listen to my explanation of why a certain way of solving certain equations worked and another did not, she exclaimed: "I appreciate what you are trying to do, but I don't need or want to know why the method works! All I need to know is how to follow the steps that the teacher wants and get the answers that she wants." This was an A student.

Students recognize that it would be impossible to delve deeply into their school subjects, even if they wanted to. Time does not permit it. They must follow the schedule set by the school curriculum. Moreover, many of them have become convinced that they must also engage in a certain number of formal extracurricular activities, to prove that they are the "well rounded" individuals that top colleges are seeking. Anyone who really allowed himself or herself to pursue a love of one subject would fail all the others. To succeed, students must acquire just the limited information and shallow understanding that is needed to perform well on the tests; anything beyond that is wasted time. All of the top students learn that lesson.

In many cases the rules about what is and isn't cheating in school are arbitrary and have nothing to do with learning. If you create a summary sheet of the terms and facts relevant to a test and then consult that sheet while taking the test, you have cheated. However, if you create such a sheet and commit it to a form of short-term memory that lasts just long enough for the test and then vanishes, you have not cheated. If you create a term paper by copying out large chunks of other people's writing and pasting them together, that is cheating; but if you do essentially the same thing and then paraphrase sufficiently rather than use the copied paragraphs exactly, that is not cheating.

Students understand that the rules distinguishing cheating from not cheating in school are like the rules of a game. But in this case it's a game that they did not choose to play. They are forced to go to school, forced to do the assignments, forced to take the tests. They have little or no say in what they study, how they are tested, or the rules concerning what is or isn't cheating. Under these conditions, it's hard to respect the rules.

Teachers often say that if you cheat in school you are only cheating yourself, because you are shortcutting your own education. But that argument holds water only if what you would have learned by not cheating outweighs the value of whatever you did with the time you saved by cheating. If, by cheating in Subject X you gain more time to really learn Subject Y—which you care about, and which may or may not be a school subject—then have you really shortcut your education by cheating?

In my experience talking with students, the argument against cheating that makes most sense to them is the argument that by cheating they are hurting students who didn't cheat (but they correctly add that this argument applies primarily in those rare cases where the teacher grades on a curve). They see the "system" as an enemy and hold few qualms about cheating to beat it, but they generally don't see other students as enemies, and so they feel bad if they think their cheating hurts other students.

In fact, one of the biggest reasons why cheaters are sometimes caught is that they share their cheating with other students, and somewhere in the sharing the word leaks out to school officials. For example, a student who steals a copy of an upcoming test shares the copy with everyone in the class, and then someone tells the teacher. The problems that arise from the "students versus the system" attitude that schools promote are serious and endless. The honest student, who reports the cheating, becomes a ratfink.

In other respects, cheating to get high grades seems to many students to be a win-win-win situation. They want to get high grades, their parents want them to get high grades, and their teachers want them to get high grades. Teachers generally don't look hard to see cheating and often ignore it when they do see it, because the higher grades—especially on standardized tests—make them (the teachers) look good too. And many parents, far from deploring their children's cheating, are ready to go to court to fight any school officials who dare make an accusation of cheating.

Cheating is Rampant in Schools, Especially Among the "Best" Students

Not surprisingly, surveys show that cheating is very common in schools. In fact, if "normal" means what most people do, then school cheating is normal. On anonymous questionnaires, as many as 98 percent of students admit to some form of cheating and roughly 70 percent admit to repeated acts of the most blatant forms of cheating, such as copying whole tests from other students or plagiarizing whole papers. When asked in such surveys why cheating occurs, many students give the kinds of answers that I just discussed in the paragraphs above. When asked whether they consider cheating in school to be a serious moral offense, many if not most say no. The rates of cheating and reasons given for it are pretty consistent at all levels of formal education, at least from middle school on through college (for summaries of surveys, see McMahon, 2007; Olek, 2008; Hot Topics in Education, 2011).

The surveys also reveal an overall increase in the amount of cheating in recent years and a shift in who does most of it. In times past, the most frequent cheaters were the "poor students," who cheated out of desperation just to pass. Today, however, the highest incidences of cheating are among the "best students," the ones destined for the top colleges and graduate schools. As one high-school graduate put it in a call-in to an NPR program on school cheating, "I was in honors classes in high school because I wanted to get into the best schools, and all of us in those classes cheated; we needed the grades to get into the best schools." (Pytel, 2007.)

Apparently the "best" students today are driven as much by their own sense of desperation as poor students were in the past. They feel that they must get top grades and get into the top schools or else they will let everyone down who is important to them, including their parents and themselves. Not getting into the top schools is, to them, out and out failure.

These are kids who are smart and hardworking, who would do well even without cheating, but who cheat to get the extra edge they feel they need to be seen as truly the best. They are like Barry Bonds or Roger Clemens taking steroids.

And, then, some of those top students choose science as a career.

The Continuity Between Cheating in School and Cheating in Science

Let's take the (hypothetical) example of Bob, who decides at some point in college to go on to become a scientist. He makes this decision not because he really loves science or has some burning questions that he wants to answer through scientific methods. His own sense of curiosity was drilled out of him long ago by the tedium of school. Rather, he decides to become a scientist because (a) he has always done well in science classes (only partly by cheating), (b) others have encouraged him to become a scientist, and (c) he sees that scientists have relatively high status and he would like that. In his gut, he doesn't really quite even know what it means to be a scientist, but he thinks it would be a good career.

So, Bob applies to and gets accepted into a graduate program in science leading to a PhD. Now, as a graduate student, he is in some sense "doing" science, as he carries out the research he must do for his doctoral dissertation. But is it "real" science, or is he still a student going through hoops? He finds that as he works on his research project—a project that was designed more by his advisor than by himself—he is not getting quite the results that his advisor expected. The advisor seems disappointed and is lavishing much more attention and praise on another PhD candidate who is getting strong, positive, publishable results.

Bob gets worried about his future. He's working hard and, through no fault of his own, it's not paying off. So, the old habit of cheating returns. By manipulating just a few numbers, in some of his data sets, he turns statistically insignificant results into significant ones—results that lead to a much-praised dissertation and to a number of publications in prestigious scientific journals.

Bob has many ways to rationalize this cheating to himself. His advisor assigned him to a bum project; the laboratory conditions were not adequate for getting the expected results; the numbers he changed came from observations that may have been flukes; and he had to do this because otherwise his whole career was in jeopardy. The problem is that now his cheating has serious consequences. Bob may see himself as just doing what he had to do to go through another hoop, but others see his work as a serious scientific contribution. Every act of cheating in science pokes a hole in the scientific enterprise. Science absolutely depends upon honesty. Bob cheats because (a) he feels pressure to cheat, (b) he feels he's still really a student and not yet a scientist, and (c) he has a long history of cheating as a student and rationalizing that cheating.

And where does this end for Bob? At what point will he be done with hoops and become a "real scientist," motivated solely by the search for truth? When Bob becomes a postdoctoral fellow working in someone else's lab, he is still in some ways a student, still needing to prove himself so he can get a real job. Then, when he becomes an assistant professor in a university science department, there are still hoops to go through. He must publish research articles in respected journals in order to get tenure. It's "up or out" after seven years as assistant professor, and now Bob has a young family to support and "out" is not, in his mind, an option. The pressure to cheat may now be even stronger than before. And suppose he does get tenure. By this time the habit of cheating has become rather fixed. It has worked all along. Moreover, by now he has his own graduate students, and to support them he must get grants. Also by now he has a high reputation, which he enjoys in spite of his uneasy knowledge that it is not entirely deserved. To keep getting grants, to keep supporting his students, and to keep up that high reputation, he must continue getting strong, publishable, positive results. The hoops never end.

One of the tragedies of our system of schooling is that it deflects students from discovering what they truly love and find worth doing for its own sake. Instead, it teaches them that life is a series of hoops that one must get through, by one means or another, and that success lies in others' judgments rather than in real, self-satisfying accomplishments. Fortunately, most people manage to get off of that track, or largely off of it, once they leave school and begin to enjoy more freedom of choice. But some never get off of it; they are perpetually like students, constantly striving to impress others in ways that lead them through one hoop after another. Some of those become cheaters in science—or in business, or law, or politics, or. . . .

References

Fanelli, W. (2009). How many scientists fabricate and falsify research? A systematic review and meta-analysis of survey data. *PLoS One*, 4 (#5), 1-11.

McMahon, R. (2007). Everybody does it: Academic cheating is at an all-time high. *San Francisco Chronicle*, Sept. 9, 2007.

Oleck, J. (2008). Most high-school students admit to cheating. School Library Journal, March 10, 2008.

Pytel, B. (2007). Cheating is on the rise. http://classroom-issues. suite101.com/article.cfm/cheating_is_on_the_rise, Sept. 16, 2007.

Seventy-five to 98 percent of college students have cheated. *Hot Topics in Education*, June, 2011. https://study.com/articles/75_ to_98_Percent_of_College_Students_Have_Cheated.html.

Wade, N. Harvard researcher may have fabricated data. *New York Times*, Aug. 27, 2010.

7

ADHD and School

*Assessing Normalcy in an
Abnormal Environment*

*ADHD diagnoses derive from schools'
intolerance of normal human diversity.*

JULY 7, 2010

According to the most authoritative recent data, approximately eight percent of children in the United States, aged 4 to 17, have been diagnosed as having ADHD (Attention Deficit Hyperactivity Disorder) (Visser et al., 2007; CDC, 2005; Mayes et al, 2009). The same reports note that the disorder is about three times as frequent in boys as it is in girls, so this means that roughly 12 percent of boys and four percent of girls have received the diagnosis. Think of it. Twelve percent of boys—that's approximately one boy out of every eight—has been determined by some clinical authority, using official diagnostic criteria set out by the American Psychiatric Association, to have this particular mental disorder! [Note added in June 2015: Things have gotten worse. According to new data, now 11 percent of children overall and 20 percent of boys are diagnosed with ADHD at some point in their school career—see Schwarz and Cohen, New York Times, March 31, 2013.]

If only teachers' ratings were used, the numbers would be even greater. In one study involving 16 different schools and more than 3,000 children, teachers filled out the standard ADHD diagnostic checklist of behaviors for the students in their classrooms (Nolan et al., 2001). In that study, where teachers' ratings were not averaged in with the ratings made by parents, 23 percent of elementary school boys and 20 percent of secondary school boys were diagnosed as having ADHD. What an amazing finding. By teachers' ratings, nearly one-fourth of all elementary school boys and one-fifth of all secondary school boys has the mental disorder, ADHD!

ADHD is Fundamentally a School Adjustment Problem

What does it mean to have ADHD? Largely, it means failure to adapt to the conditions of standard schooling. Most diagnoses of ADHD originate with teachers' observations (Mayes et al., 2009). In the typical case, a child has been a persistent pain in the neck in school—not paying attention, not completing assignments, disrupting class with excessive movements and verbal outbursts—and the teacher, consequently, urges the parents to consult with a clinician about the possibility that the child has ADHD. Using the standard diagnostic checklists, the clinician then takes into account the ratings of teachers and of parents concerning the child's behavior. If the ratings meet the criterion level, then a diagnosis of ADHD is made. The child may then be put on a drug such as Adderall or Concerta, with the result, usually, that the child's behavior in school improves. The student begins to do what the teacher asks him to do; the classroom is less disrupted; and the parents are relieved. The drug "works."

The diagnostic criteria for ADHD, as outlined by DSM-IV (the official diagnostic manual of the American Psychiatric Association), clearly pertain primarily to school behavior. The manual lists nine criteria having to do with inattention and another nine having to do with hyperactivity and impulsivity. If a child manifests at least six of either set of nine, to a sufficient degree and over a long enough period of time, then the child is identified as having one or another version of ADHD. Depending on which set of criteria is most manifested, the child is given a diagnosis of ADHD Predominantly Inattentive Type; ADHD Predominantly Hyperactive-Impulsive Type; or ADHD Combined Type.

Here, for you to peruse, are the complete lists of criteria, quoted directly from DSM-IV*:

----

*In order to make ADHD not appear to be just a school problem, DSM-IV adds the stipulation that the symptoms must be seen in at least one other setting, not just in school. However, it does not stipulate that the other setting has to be radically different from school. It is easy to see how parents, after being convinced that their child has ADHD from the school reports, might "see" such symptoms at home or in another setting—especially while doing homework, or when involved in some adult-directed activity such as lessons or formal sports outside of school. Nevertheless, the fail-

Inattention

1. Often does not give close attention to details or makes careless mistakes in schoolwork, work, or other activities.
2. Often has trouble keeping attention on tasks or play activities.
3. Often does not seem to listen when spoken to directly.
4. Often does not follow instructions and fails to finish schoolwork, chores, or duties in the workplace (not due to oppositional behavior or failure to understand instructions).
5. Often has trouble organizing activities.
6. Often avoids, dislikes, or doesn't want to do things that take a lot of mental effort for a long period of time (such as schoolwork or homework).
7. Often loses things needed for tasks and activities (e.g., toys, school assignments, pencils, books, or tools).
8. Is often easily distracted.
9. Is often forgetful in daily activities.

Hyperactivity and Impulsivity

1. Often fidgets with hands or feet or squirms in seat.
2. Often gets up from seat when remaining in seat is expected.

---

ure of these symptoms to manifest themselves so much in settings outside of school probably explains why rates of ADHD diagnoses based just on teacher reports are so much higher than those based on a combination of teachers' and parents' reports.

3. Often runs about or climbs when and where it is not appropriate (adolescents or adults may feel very restless).

4. Often has trouble playing or enjoying leisure activities quietly.

5. Is often "on the go" or often reacts as if "driven by a motor."

6. Often talks excessively.

7. Often blurts out answers before questions have been finished.

8. Often has trouble waiting one's turn.

9. Often interrupts or intrudes on others (e.g., butts into conversations or games).

OK, after reading this list, who is not surprised that so many boys have been diagnosed as having ADHD and that teachers usually initiate the diagnostic process? Raise your hand (but please don't blurt out your answer before I call on you).

How convenient that we have this official way of diagnosing kids who don't sit still in their seats, often fail to pay attention to the teacher, don't regularly do their school assignments, often speak out of turn, and blurt out answers before the questions are finished. They used to be called "naughty"—sometimes with a frown, sometimes with a smile of recognition that "kids will be kids" or "boys will be boys"—but now we "know" that they are, for biological reasons, mentally disordered. And, wonder of wonders, we even have an effective treatment. We can give them a powerful drug—a preparation of methylphenidate or amphetamine, both of which have effects on the brain similar to those of cocaine (but without the euphoria) and are, for good reasons, illegal to take unless you have been diagnosed with a mental disorder and given a prescription. The drug works. The children become more tractable and classroom management becomes easier.

The most common subtype of ADHD is the Predominantly Inattentive Type. This is the disorder that used to be called just ADD. A highly respected pediatrician at Yale University who treats (with drugs) many children diagnosed with this disorder made this interesting confession (Sidney Spiesel, quoted by Mayes et al., p. 12):

> A disproportionate number of children labeled 'ADHD without hyperactivity' are exceptionally bright and creative children. I've often thought that these kids find their own inner theater much richer and more interesting than the outer theater of the classroom and, so, naturally, focus on it at the expense of classroom attention. . . The proper fix for this problem would be done at the school level, a place where I am unlikely to have any significant effect. I can, however, help these children concentrate and return their attention to the classroom.

Why Do So Many Kids Have Difficulty Adjusting to School?

From an evolutionary perspective, school is an abnormal environment. Nothing like it ever existed in the long course of evolution during which we acquired our human nature.

School is a place where children are expected to spend most of their time sitting quietly in chairs, listening to a teacher talk about things that don't particularly interest them, reading what they are told to read, writing what they are told to write, and feeding memorized information back on tests. As I have detailed elsewhere (e.g., Gray, 2012, 2013), during the entire course of human history until very recently, children were in charge of their own education. They learned by following their inner, instinctive guides, which led them to pay close attention to everything around them, especially to the activities of other people, to converse with others as equal partners, to explore their world actively, and to practice the skills crucial to their culture through self-directed play in age-mixed groups.

From an evolutionary perspective, it is not at all surprising that many children fail to adapt to the school environment, in ways that lead to the ADHD diagnosis. All children have at least some difficulty adapting to school. It is not natural for children (or anyone else, for that matter) to spend so much time sitting, so much time ignoring their own real questions and interests, so much time doing precisely what they are told to do. We humans are highly adaptable, but we are not infinitely so. It is possible to push an environment so far out of the bounds of normal that many of our members just can't abide by it, and that is what we have done with schools. It is not surprising to me that the rate of diagnosis of ADHD began to skyrocket during the same decade (the 1990s) when schools became even more restrictive than they had been before—when high-stakes testing became prominent, when recesses were dropped, when teachers were told that they must teach to the standardized tests and everyone must pass or the teachers themselves might lose their jobs.

Schools' Intolerance of Normal Human Diversity

Why do some kids adapt to school better than others? The answer to that does lie in biology—normal biology, not abnormal biology. For good evolutionary reasons, members of our species vary genetically in ways that create diversity in personality. People have always lived in communities, and communities—as well as the individuals within them—benefit from diversity. It is good that some people are relatively restrained while others are more impulsive, that some are relatively passive while others are more active, that some are cautious while others are bolder, and so on. These are among the dimensions that make up normal personality. In situations where people are free, they find ways of behaving and learning that fit best with their biological nature, and through those means they make unique contributions to the communities in which they live. Normal human environments always have a variety of niches that people can occupy, and people who are free naturally choose niches where they are most comfortable and happy, the niches that match best with their biological nature.

But school, especially today, does not have a variety of niches. Everyone is expected to do the same thing, at the same time, in the same way. Everyone must pass the same tests. Some people, apparently most, have a personality that allows them to adapt sufficiently well to the school environment that they pass the tests and avoid behaving in ways that the teachers can't tolerate. School may take its toll on them, but the toll is not so obvious. The toll may manifest itself as diffuse anxiety, or moderate depression, or cynicism, or suppression of initiative and creativity, but the school system can absorb all that. Those characteristics become viewed as "normal." Unless they become really extreme, they don't get diagnoses. It's the kids whose personalities do not allow them to go along with the system who get the ADHD diagnoses. And most of those are boys.

One of the biological characteristics that predisposes for ADHD in the school environment, obviously, is the Y chromosome. For evolutionary reasons, boys are, on average, more physically active, more prone to take risks, more impulsive, and less compliant than are girls. A normal distribution of such traits exists for both boys and girls. The distributions overlap considerably, but are not identical. The cutoff on the distribution that gets you a diagnosis of ADHD in our present society happens to be at a point that includes about 12 percent of boys and four percent of girls. In another setting, where they could choose their niches, most of those kids would do just fine.

An Illustrative Story

I'll conclude with a true story to illustrate all this. It pertains to a young man whom I have known well since he was 13 years old. Throughout his school years he was funny, playful, very bright, extraordinarily impulsive, and a huge pain in the neck to essentially all of his teachers. He rarely completed a school assignment and was often disruptive in class. He could not or would not focus on any of his school lessons and he seemed unable to prevent himself from saying what was on his mind rather than what he was supposed to say. His parents were regularly called in for conferences. When school officials asked his parents to take him to a clinic for ADHD diagnosis, his mother—a physician who knew that the long-term brain effects of the drugs used to treat ADHD have never been tested in humans and have proven deleterious in laboratory animals—refused to do so. The boy had all the characteristics of ADHD Combined Type, and I have no doubt that he would have received that diagnosis had his mother consented. Thanks to a relatively lenient and understanding assistant principal, he was passed along from grade to grade, even though he did almost none of the assigned work and failed most of his tests. He graduated from high school at the bottom of his class.

Then the good part of his life began. Clearly unprepared for college, he did a year in an internship program and discovered that he enjoyed cooking and was good at it. After working in a restaurant for a while, he received recommendations that got him into a culinary school, where he loved the work and excelled. Now, in his 20s, he is a very successful chef. In this setting, which requires constant, active, hands-on work and the kind of mental brilliance that involves attending to and responding to many competing and immediately demanding sources at once, he shines. He has found his niche. He learned nothing from his 13 years of public schooling, but, because of his buoyant personality, school did not destroy him. When he was finally out of school, free to pursue his own interests in the real world, he found his niche and now is thriving there. The real world, thank goodness, is very different from school!

References

Centers for Disease Control and Prevention (Sept. 2, 2005). Prevalence of diagnosis and medication treatment for ADHD. *MMWR: Morbidity and Mortality Weekly Report* 54, 842-846.

Gray, P. (2013). *Free to Learn: Why Unleashing the Instinct to Play Will Make Our Children Happier, More Self-Reliant, and Better Students for Life*. Basic Books.

Gray, P. (2012). The value of a play-filled childhood in development of the hunter-gatherer individual. In Narvaez, D., Panksepp, J., Schore, A., and Gleason, T. (Eds.), *Evolution, Early Experience and Human Development: From Research to Practice and Policy*, pp. 252-370. Oxford University Press.

Mayes, R., Bagwell, C., & Erkulwater, J. (2009). *Medicating Children: ADHD and Pediatric Mental Health*. Harvard University Press.

Nolan, E. E., Gadow, K. D., & Sprafkin, J. (2001). Teacher reports of DSM-IV ADHD, ODD, and CD symptoms in schoolchildren. *Journal of the Academy of Child and Adolescent Psychiatry*, 40, 241-249.

Visser, S. N., Lesesne, C. A., & Perou, R. (2007). National estimates and factors associated with medication treatment for childhood attention-deficit/hyperactivity Disorder. *Pediatrics*, 119, S99-S106.

8

Experiences of ADHD-Labeled Kids Who Leave Typical Schooling

Many children diagnosed with ADHD do well when allowed to take charge of their own education.

SEPTEMBER 9, 2010

Several weeks ago I posted, on my *Psychology Today* blog, a call for stories about children who have been diagnosed with ADHD (Attention Deficit Hyperactivity Disorder) and have been homeschooled, unschooled, or "free schooled." I received 28 such stories and analyzed them qualitatively.

The analysis suggests that (1) most ADHD-diagnosed kids do fine without drugs if they are not in a conventional school; (2) the ADHD characteristics don't vanish when the kids leave conventional school, but the characteristics are no longer as big a problem as they were before; and (3) ADHD-diagnosed kids seem to do especially well when they are allowed to take charge of their own education. In what follows

I will elaborate and illustrate each of these conclusions with quotations from the stories. But, first, here are some numbers concerning whom the stories were about and who wrote them.

Of the 28 stories:

- 19 were about boys and nine were about girls;

- 26 were written by a parent of the ADHD-diagnosed child; the other two were written, respectively, by the diagnosed person himself (who was 24 years old at the time he wrote) and by an older sister of the diagnosed person;

- 24 were about children who were diagnosed with ADHD through a formal clinical procedure and the other four were about children who were labeled by medical or school officials as "ADHD" but whose parents, while agreeing that the child showed the full set of ADHD characteristics, chose not to proceed with formal diagnosis;

- 21 were about children who started their education in a conventional school and then left conventional schooling; the other seven were about children who had never attended a conventional school;

- 21 described their nonconventional schooling as homeschooling, five described theirs as unschooling, and two described theirs as alternative schooling (one was described as a small private school in a home, "similar to homeschooling," and the other as a school "loosely based on Sudbury Valley").

And now, here are the three conclusions, along with some of the quotations that led to each.

Conclusion 1: Most children who had been medicated for ADHD while in conventional schooling were taken off of medication when removed from conventional schooling, and those who were never in conventional schooling were never medicated.

Research studies have regularly revealed that most children who attend a conventional school and are diagnosed with ADHD take stimulant drugs (dopamine reuptake inhibitors) as treatment (e.g., Mayes et al, 2009). That was not the case for this sample of ADHD-labeled children outside of conventional school. Of the 28 children in this sample, 13 were never medicated (these were mostly children who were never in a conventional school or who were removed from conventional school very shortly after the diagnosis), nine were medicated for at least part of the time that they had been in a conventional school but were removed from medication after removal from school, and only six (21 percent of the full sample) were medicated at the time the story was written. Of those six, one was on Strattera (a non-stimulant norepinephrine reuptake inhibitor), one had just started his first day of homeschooling and was taking Vyvanse (a stimulant), and the remaining four were still on stimulants even though they had been homeschooled for a year or more.

Here is a sample of comments made concerning children who had been removed from conventional school and taken off of stimulants (each bulleted comment concerns a different family and child):

▪ "We decided [when he was in third grade in public school] to switch from Strattera to Adderall. We tried various doses but weren't getting what we needed, so we tried Vyvanse and Concerta at various doses. They just weren't working for him. There seemed to be a short-term improvement, or at least a perceived improvement but it really didn't fix the problem. In all this, his anxiety was paralyzing, so, of course, we ended up on Prozac. . . . As parents, it was exactly where we didn't want to be, having a drugged kid just to keep him in school. . . . he was being pulled from class daily for being disruptive—making noises, interrupting teachers, asking to leave. He and his special ed. teacher were in constant battle. After a particularly ugly IEP we pulled the plug. We finished the year with homeschooling and he made more progress in three months than he had made in three years of traditional public school. We continued with the meds for another month or so but discontinued them from that point on."

▪ "My little brother was put on ADD medication at the age of 7, because he was not able to focus well in school or in his martial arts classes. I saw his personality immediately dull when they put him on the drugs, but he was much better able to function in organized learning settings. When he was 15, though, he took himself off of the meds, and only then did he realize, and begin to vocalize, that he had been having paranoid delusions for years as a result of the medications. As a 10-year-old, he was terrified during every shower because he thought terrorists were poisoning the water. My brother wasn't so disruptive on the medications, but he never excelled in school until his last two years of high school, when he attended a private school that was loosely based on Sudbury Valley. Now, he is a fantastic musician, is attending college, and has never had any more problems with delusions or paranoia. He hates the drugs he was put on and has a lot of lingering anger about it to this day."

■ "At age 8½ we decided to try Adderall, because he was struggling with attention and learning. He developed severe depression at age 10 [while on Adderall]. He was placed on a few more drugs. Each drug seemed to make him better for a few months, and then worse. When a drug caused a side effect, he would be given another one to combat the side effect. . . . He developed a B12 deficit because of the Adderall. This gave him obsessive-compulsive behaviors, and we had to give him B12 injections. . . . Then [after altering his diet and removing toxins from his environment] we weaned him off of the Adderall. There was no difference in his focus or activity at that point. He was/is fine. We continue to homeschool him. . . . It was just the best thing we could have done for our child. He is now 16 and planning to go to college."

■ "By fourth grade [this time a private school with an advanced curriculum] her seven teachers wanted her tested. We tried Ritalin for a few months, but it only resulted in a daytime compliant zombie that wanted to work even harder at night to pursue her knowledge. By spring they asked for a conference and refunded our deposit for the coming year. . . . They agreed she was a classroom management problem, because she could do anything but listen." [The story goes on to describe the success of homeschooling, without drugs, and the fact that she has been accepted to a four-year college.]

▪ "Now that we are homeschooling (and he is thriving academically, socially, and behaviorally), medication is no longer a subject of consideration. We are excited about homeschooling—it has changed our lives for the better; we have our son back."

▪ [Concerning a boy who had been on various drugs in third and fourth grades in public school after a previous period of homeschooling without drugs:] "We pulled him out of school and went back to homeschooling. I took him off the meds to get a baseline on his behavior. Things improved for him so quickly that I never restarted Rx medications."

▪ "As a child, around age 5, I was diagnosed with ADHD. I was put on Ritalin and continued on the drug until the age of 11. After coming off the drug my parents noted that I was less angry and generally happier with what was going on around me, as well as less prone to tantrums. At the end of fifth grade my parents made the choice to homeschool me. I was homeschooled from grades six to 10 [without drugs] and during that time I pulled ahead in my math work and got As on all of my tests. I was able to study how I wanted to, fidget when I wanted to. . . . Then [beginning with grade 11] I was returned to school [for some but not all courses]. . . . I was then put back on a new form of Ritalin. We tried it for a month, and I went into a severe depression from the effects. After a month I was pulled back off it and that was the end of talks about drugs for the condition. . . . I am now 24, married, and expecting a child. I went to college after my senior year . . . and joined the Guard. I have noticed in the course of my life that I am calmer for the most part now. I still have urges, . . . not what I consider bad urges, but urges to say what is on my mind and to express an opinion whenever I can. . . . Overall, I am happy. I love my life, my wife and my family.

In contrast to these quotations, those who kept their child on a stimulant after starting homeschooling reported the drug to be helpful. Here are the three most positive pro-drug comments:

▪ "We tried Concerta, but he went crazy. Eventually we tried Strattera [a non-stimulant ADHD medication, a norepinephrine reuptake inhibitor] and it helped so much. He now has that second to think about what he's going to do and he makes better choices. No more temper tantrums, throwing things, hitting, or reckless behavior."

▪ "Off meds she is inattentive, argumentative, and unpleasant to be with. On meds she is productive, fun, and kind. She does have the side effect of appetite suppression, so we have to get creative to get enough calories into her. That is easily accommodated, though, and we have been happy with her progress both socially and academically in the three years that we have homeschooled."

▪ "Once the drug [Focalin XR, a stimulant] kicked in, everything changed. He not only grasped concepts, he remembered them. He flew through three years of math in six months. He will start high school in the fall, with over 20 hours of high school credit, and honors level high school science under his belt [from his homeschooling years]. He is becoming the brilliant kid I only saw in flashes before the drugs."

Conclusion 2: The children's behavior, moods, and learning generally improved when they stopped conventional schooling, not because their ADHD characteristics vanished but because they were now in a situation where they could learn to deal with those characteristics.

Only two or three of the respondents reported that the ADHD-like behavior disappeared when the child was removed from conventional school. The great majority said or implied that such characteristics remained but were no longer such a big problem, primarily because, out of school, the child could be active and self-directed without being disruptive and had opportunities to learn how to cope with his or her personality characteristics. Here are some relevant quotations:

▪ "He learns fine as long as he is moving. I have the feeling that in a formal mass education setting, the focus would still be on getting him to sit still. As it is, he would be entering eighth grade in the local government school, but he's doing sophomore/junior level work and even has some AP credits. He's teaching himself German and Latin because he wants to. I have no desire to squelch his joy of learning just to get him to sit still! . . . He's well adjusted socially and behaves appropriately. However, when he's with other kids with ADHD, we notice they sort of snowball each other's behaviors."

▪ "She is a terrific free-range learner. She is sometimes afraid that she is 'behind' and will find websites and books describing what she should know and just devour them. She was reading on an eighth-grade level at third grade three years ago, so she's reading somewhere on a high school level now. . . . Her behavior is normally excellent. Sometimes she has outbursts of exuberance that can be both inconsiderate and difficult to stop, like running through the house shouting late at night."

▪ "I think the real advantage of homeschooling has been in the development of my son's social skills. He is a thoroughly nice person, both kind and empathetic. I just don't see how he could have learned to socialize as well at a school where he was being made to feel that he was unacceptable all day."

▪ [Concerning a boy who at age 5 was diagnosed with ADHD, Sensory Integration Dysfunction, and Pervasive Developmental Disorder and who began homeschooling shortly after that:] "Today [at nearly age 16] he is an articulate, outgoing and confident young man. He takes no medication . . . has no odd behaviors . . . and impresses every adult he meets. . . . His learning style is nothing that could ever be harnessed in the classroom. He almost intuits how to fix everything from cars to air conditioners to . . ." [This writer goes on to describe how her son is preparing himself for a career through apprenticeships in the trades and at an antique store, in ways that would not have been possible in school.]

■ "His anxiety is gone [since leaving public school and starting homeschooling]. As far as schooling goes, he definitely has a hard time completing his work. He is indeed easily distracted. . . . He's still impulsive and demanding but we can handle it much better than the school could and we're all less stressed for it. He takes some classes through local groups and museums and still has a hard time attending to the teachers, but he manages now that it isn't an all-day everyday prospect."

■ "My son's friendships are always volatile. While he loves being with them, his tendency to 'lose it' or be 'hyper' often gets him into scrapes and he will quite often fall out with them. Being out of school has allowed him to walk away when this happens, to come home, reflect on the situation, talk about it and to not engage in the downward spiral of anger and resentment through being with them all day every day. He is learning about life, about life skills and, most importantly, how to be a happy and fulfilled adult."

■ "Her public school years of K-3 were mostly disastrous. . . . In response to repeated encouragement by the resource teacher, when she was in third grade we took her to a psychologist and came home with a diagnosis of ADHD and a prescription for Metadate. We tried it for about a week, and the testing results did show a noticeable improvement in areas such as short-term memory (from 0/10 to 5/10 on one test, for example). Nevertheless, we couldn't bring ourselves to continue the meds: She was awake until very late at night, had a glazed look in her eyes, developed a small rash on her thighs, etc. . . . Instead we started her for fourth grade in a small private alternative school for grades K-7/8. It has about 14 or 15 kids and is like a big home-schooled family. . . . Getting her out of public school was the best decision we could have made. . . . And as for us as parents: Before we bailed out for the world of alternative schooling, we felt like we were raising not a child, but rather a set of problems in need of a set of solutions. No more."

"We started homeschooling in kindergarten. It was a disaster. Sitting down for 10 minutes a day for a lesson was like pulling teeth. She would weep and cry that she hated school. 'Do you hate stories?' No. 'Do you hate games?' No. 'What do you hate?' Sitting DOWNNNNN! (Wail). I persevered through kindergarten, but with nothing to show for progress after a year of trying. For first grade I modified my style a little and let her do things like play Legos, doodle, or 'sew' while we read. It helped a little. . . . By second grade I had given up. . . . She was not learning to read. . . .. Then one day I walked in and she was reading *The Chronicles of Narnia*. It had just clicked, at around age 8. . . . She still misspells atrociously. And her behavior in groups can still be very wild—she is so excitable and dramatic and sometimes scares other children a little. . . . As I've gotten to know her better, I find it more and more odd that we label these children 'learning disabled.' She does naturally the things other children find so hard—word problems in math, seeing large complex solutions to problems, being a creative problem solver, having a unique perspective on a book she read. The things that are hard to teach. And she struggles with the things that are so easily remedied . . . calculators and spell-check anyone?"

Conclusion 3: Many of these children seem to have a very high need for self-direction in education, and many "hyper focus" on tasks that interest them.

A staff member who works at a school modeled after Sudbury Valley emailed me this interesting comment about kids who had been diagnosed with ADHD before coming to that school:

> The ADHD label is applied to two very different sorts of kids. One type really has 'Attention Surfeit Disorder.' Most of these get deeply involved in exactly what they want to do. . . . They do their thing—with other kids when it overlaps with other kids' interests, and without other kids when they are caught up in something that other kids aren't interested in. They get labeled ADD not because they can't attend but because they have no coping mechanisms for enforced boredom. . . . The other type are simply physically active to the point of being problematic when quiet is called for. These kids may get themselves ejected from JC [Judicial Committee] or the School Meeting when they can't control themselves, and generally have long records for Running and Roughhousing and for Disturbingly Noisy activities. A combination of not calling unduly for quiet (most of these kids can be outside running and roughhousing to their hearts' content most of the time without bugging anyone) and a fair and reasonable JC that helps these kids discern time and place makes this problem less for us and gives the kids a sense of justice and time and place that informs them and lets

them develop the ability to shift gears when quiet and serene are called for.

In the sample of stories I received, many of the kids seem to fall clearly into the first category. They seem to be kids who have an even greater need for self-direction in education than do typical kids. In this regard, it is not surprising that the few kids in this sample who were still on ADHD medications during homeschooling seemed to be primarily those whose homeschooling was structured by the parent and modeled after the education one would receive in a conventional school.

A number of the quotations that I have already presented allude to the ADHD-labeled child's need to control his or her own learning. Here are a few more:

▪ "She chooses her own subjects and learning material daily. . . . She learns much better if she can follow an interest and then hyper focus on it. She may pick something different, and seemingly unrelated, every day, and then tie that randomness into a major project that she will work on for a month."

▪ "It seems to be a matter of interest. If he is into something he will be focused and attentive for long stretches, if not he gets antsy. As an example, at our local homeschool conference a robotics club had a booth and had a robot there. My son would have stayed there asking questions about the robot for the rest of the afternoon if I had not moved him along."

▪ "We've been unschooling for several years now. He is 11. . . . He is energetic and rambunctious at times, but often finds an interest that holds his attention for hours on end. The only time he fits the ADHD diagnosis is when he is bored or uninterested in something. Or he will be particularly rambunctious after sitting for long periods of time."

▪ "After a while [of parent-directed homeschooling] it became impossible for him to learn. His anxiety increased to a level that we were forced to allow him to take anti-anxiety drugs, which he did for a few months. . . . I then stumbled on self-directed learning/unschooling and have not looked back! . . . It all made perfect sense. My son makes choices about what he wants to learn, he makes his own decisions about when and how he will learn it, he has learnt to define his own boundaries and takes responsibility for his own learning. If he is interested in something, we facilitate and provide resources, links, take him to places that supply the stuff he needs. He has taken a huge interest in music technology. . . . He has produced some amazing music, he has found out about a variety of things he is interested in, he has self-defined interests. . . . He is wise, and he knows what choices to follow more than we do. Never would I have believed last year, when everything was so bleak and traumatic, that a year on, everything would be looking so rosy, and so absolutely fascinating as we follow just what it means to give your child the freedom to be themselves."

▪ "Our homeschooling started out with a curriculum program that she hated following. She would just want to read all of the history book. . . . The piecemeal, parsing out of knowledge that is 'curriculum' always galled her. We started un-schooling and everything fell into place. . . . The 'problem' is that she loves knowledge, wants to go at her own pace (fast), ignoring some subjects while pursuing others, and delving into specialized interests no one else her age has."

▪ "We began unschooling about four years ago. . . . Today she's 14½ years old. . . . She is creative, responsible, fun to be around. She has no trouble reading and is skilled at using math in her everyday life. . . . She has no signs of the problems the school district saw in her when she was 9 years old. . . . She was in a large, chaotic class with several children who required one-on-one aides, the district was in the first year of imple-menting Everyday Math (which I called Everyday Crying), and the books they were giving the children to read, IMO, were boring. Tests made her anxious and she was overloaded sensorily by the noise and smells at the school, especially in the cafeteria. Since she's been home she's just bloomed. People who know her find it hard to believe that anyone ever ques-tioned her intelligence or ability to focus. She's smarter and more responsible than many adults I know."

In concluding, I should say that this is obviously just a preliminary study. It is, however, as far as I can tell, the only study that anyone has conducted to date concerning ADHD-diagnosed children's abilities to learn, and to cope without drugs, outside of the conventional school environment. My hope is that this preliminary study will draw the attention of the research community so that more formal, large-scale studies will be conducted. As a culture we are so used to thinking of school as the normal environment for children that we rarely even consider the possibility of children learning and developing well outside of that environment. I am very grateful to those who responded to my call for stories and took the time to write out, so clearly, the experiences of their ADHD-labeled son or daughter.

Reference

Mayes, R., Bagwell, C., & Erkulwater, J. (2009). *Medicating Children: ADHD and Pediatric Mental Health*. Harvard University Press.

9

How Does School Wound?

Kirsten Olson Has Counted Some Ways

*Dr. Kirstin Olson's interviews identified
seven kinds of school wounds*

JUNE 28, 2011

Let me introduce you to Dr. Kirsten Olson. She is an educational researcher, activist, consultant, and writer deeply concerned about children, learning, and the conditions of our schools. She is, among other things, president of the board of directors of IDEA (the Institute for Democratic Education in America). I met her for the first time, for lunch and conversation, a couple of weeks ago, and then I eagerly read her book, *Wounded by School: Recapturing the Joy in Learning and Standing up to Old School Culture.* If you have ever gone to school, or have a child in school, or might someday have a child in school, or care about children in school, I recommend her book to you.

Wounded by School is the outcome of research that Olson

began when she was an education doctoral candidate at Harvard. As one who loves learning and has always had high esteem for education, Olson intended to conduct research into the delights and enlightenment experienced in the course of schooling. But when she began interviewing people to learn about such positive effects, she found that they talked instead about the pain of school. Here is how Olson's doctoral advisor, Sara Laurence-Lightfoot, put it in a forward to the book:

> In her first foray into the field—in-depth interviews with an award-winning architect, a distinguished professor, a gifted writer, a marketing executive—Olson certainly expected to hear stories of joyful and productive learning, stories that mixed seriousness, adventure, and pleasure, work and play, desire and commitment. Instead, she discovered the shadows of pain, disappointment, even cynicism in their vivid recollections of schooling. Instead of the light that she expected, she found darkness. And their stories did not merely refer to old wounds now healed and long forgotten; they recalled deeply embedded wounds that still bruised and ached, wounds that still compromised and distorted their sense of themselves as persons and professionals.

As her project expanded, Olson began interviewing people of all ages, from schoolchildren on up to grandparents, people from a wide range of socioeconomic backgrounds and occupying a wide variety of careers. She was struck by the earnestness and emotion that came forth as people talked about the wounds that they still felt in relation to their schooling.

Olson was pioneering a direct way to understand the effects of school on psychological development. She asked people who had been there how school affected them.

In her book, Olson categorizes the wounds into seven groups, and she illustrates each with quotations from interviews. Then, in later chapters, she describes how caring parents, teachers, and students themselves can help prevent and heal the wounds. Here I'll simply list and describe in my own words Olson's seven categories. (I've added my own twist to the description of each type of wound, so if you find fault in the descriptions, the fault may be mine rather than Olson's.)

The first four categories of wounds all seem to result primarily from the restrictions that are placed on students' behavior and learning in school—the preset curriculum, the narrow set of permissible learning procedures, the tests in which there is one right answer for every question, and the often arbitrary rules that students have no role in creating. These categories are:

1. Wounds of creativity. School stifles creativity. This is perhaps the most obvious wound of school. Students' own passions and interests are generally ignored. Students' unique, creative ways of solving problems and their outside-the-box answers to questions, which fail to match the teachers' answer sheets, are not understood and are graded as wrong by busy teachers. Rote learning and tests that have one right answer for every question leave no room for creativity. Olson's informants who went on to live creative lives apparently did so despite, not because of, schooling. They had to recover or rebuild the creative spirit that had been so natural to them

before starting school. My own guess is that altogether too many others rarely think about creativity once they have lost it in school; they may not even notice this wound. And then there are those who remain creative in those realms that school doesn't touch, but become uncreative in the realms covered by the school curriculum. How many people have totally lost mathematical or scientific creativity because of the ways these are taught in school?

2. Wounds of compliance. In school students must continuously follow rules and procedures that they have no role in creating and must complete assignments that make no sense in terms of their own learning needs. Students generally cannot question these rules and assignments; if they do they are smart-alecks, or worse. To avoid getting into trouble, they learn to obey blindly, and in the process they learn to be bad citizens in a democracy. Democracy requires citizens who question the rules and insist on changing those that are unfair or don't make sense. They also hurt themselves by going through life following narrower paths than they might if school had not taught them that it is dangerous to explore the edges.

3. Wounds of rebellion. Some students respond to the arbitrary rules and assignments by rebelling rather than complying. They may in some cases feel intense anger toward the system that has taken away their freedom and dignity, toward teachers who seem to be complicit with that system, and toward the goody-goody students who go along. They may manifest their scorn by sitting in the back of the classroom, making snide remarks, blatantly flouting rules, and rarely if ever completing

assignments. Rebellion may sometimes be a healthier response than compliance, but if it goes too far it may hurt even more than compliance. Failure in school may cut off valued future paths. Anger toward schooling can lead to a turning away from all forms of learning. And, perhaps most tragically, the rebellion can take forms that physically harm the self and others, especially if the person turns to drugs, promiscuous sex, or crime as a form of self-expression and self-identity.

4. Wounds of numbness. The constant grind of school, doing one tedious assignment after another according to the school's schedule, following the school's procedures, can lead to intellectual numbness. Many of Olson's respondents described themselves as "zoned out" or "intellectually numb" as long as they were in school. Intellectual excitement is rarely rewarded in school, but doggedly grinding it out, doing what you are supposed to do, never missing a deadline, is rewarded. Brilliant work in one subject at the expense of ignoring another might earn you an A and an F in the two classes; but good-enough, non-inspired work in both subjects might earn you an A in both. This is one of the many ways by which schooling kills intellectual enthusiasm. When students do demonstrate enthusiasm, it is usually about something that has nothing to do with their lessons.

The remaining three categories of wounds identified by Olson all seem to be inflicted by the ways that people are ranked and sorted in school. You can be wounded differently depending on whether you are ranked low, high, or middling.

5. Wounds of underestimation. In her interviews Olson found that some described ways in which they were wounded

by assumptions made about them because of their race, social class, gender, or performance on one or another test that was supposed to measure intelligence or aptitude. In some cases, it seemed easier to go along with the assumption than to fight it, so the assumption became a self-fulfilling prophecy. More generally, a low grade achieved in a course or set of courses can unduly discourage people from following what had been their dream. A would-be biologist chooses a less-desired track because of a D in 10th-grade biology (which is completely unrelated to what real biologists do). A would-be author concludes that professional writing is beyond her scope because an English teacher could not see the sparkle of her essays or the brilliance in her non-conventional sentence structure and gave her below-average grades. If only students knew how many great achievers in our society received poor school grades in the subject of their achievement! If only teachers knew.

6. Wounds of perfectionism. High grades and high scores on intelligence tests, too, can wound. Students who develop identities as high achievers may feel extraordinary pressure to continue high achievement, in everything. For them, even an A- in a course, or getting only the second best part in the class play, or rejection by an Ivy League college, may feel like terrible failure—failure to live up to the image that others have of them, or the image they have of themselves. The wound of perfectionism explains why so many "top" students cheat, when they feel that they must to get the grade that everyone expects them to get. When grades are the measure of perfection, everything is done for the grade. In school, "perfection" and intellectual numbness are quite compatible. For an ex-

cellent description of how the wound of perfectionism can interfere with real education, I refer you to the courageous valedictory speech by Erica Goldstein (2010) on her graduation from high school.

7. Wounds of the average. The middling student, who is neither sinking nor soaring in the eyes of the school officials, may suffer from invisibility. In Olson's interviews, these people described themselves as feeling insignificant, as people who don't really matter much. In the worst cases, they developed self-identities as people who are unimportant, who do not make waves, who go along but never lead.

How unnecessary all this is! Education, as I have explained before, does not require an imposed curriculum, or forced assignments, or grading and ranking. In settings where students direct their own learning, each person has his or her own unique interests and sets of skills and weaknesses. There is no uniform scale on which to rank some as better or worse than others. That kind of school is much more like the real world than is the standard school that we have been talking about here. In the real world we need all kinds of people, all kinds of unique talents and personalities, to make things work and to make life fun.

Reference

Goldson, E. (2010). Here I stand: Coxsackie-Athens High School Valedictory Speech 2010. Downloaded at http://americaviaerica.blogspot.com/2010/07/coxsackie-athens-valedictorian-speech.html

10

They Dream of School, and None of the Dreams are Good

In this survey, 128 adults described their recurring dreams of being in school

JUNE 29, 2016

Dreams of being in school are common among adults of all ages. In fact, in dream surveys, being in school typically ranks among the top five dream categories in frequency, even among adults who have been out of school for decades (e.g., Mathes et al., 2014). In those studies, participants simply marked, on a check list, the topics they had dreamed about. Such studies tell us nothing about the nature of the dreams.

Are school dreams pleasant or unpleasant? What happens in the dreams? To address these questions, I used my last blog post to conduct an informal survey. I asked readers to describe, in the comments section, any recurring dreams they have about being in school and to indicate how pleasant or unpleasant the dreams typically are, when they last had such a dream, and how long it had been since they were a student in the type of school (elementary school, middle school, high school, or college) at which their dream is usually set.

One hundred and twenty-eight readers responded to the survey. In response to the question about the level of school involved in their dreams, 73 percent mentioned high school, 34 percent mentioned college, 12 percent elementary school, and seven percent middle school or junior high school. These totals add to more than 100 percent because some noted more than one setting for their recurring dreams. Here are the other main findings:

Nearly everyone rated their school dreams as unpleasant; nobody rated them as pleasant.

I asked people to rate the pleasantness of their recurring dream on a scale of 1 to 5, with 1 = very pleasant, 2 = somewhat pleasant, 3 = neither pleasant nor unpleasant, or equally pleasant and unpleasant, 4 = somewhat unpleasant, 5 = very unpleasant.

None of the respondents rated their recurring dream as 1 or 2. Only two respondents rated their recurring dream as a 3. One of those two rated her dream as a 3 rather than a 4 or 5 only because her "massive sense of relief" on realizing in the later part of the dream that she had already finished school negated the unpleasantness of the earlier part. All of the rest rated their school dreams as a 4 or a 5, with the average being about 4.5.

Some described their dreams as going beyond anxiety to a level they identified as panic. Here are a few quotations illustrating the intense emotions experienced:

I just keep doing circles in the hallways, trying to get to classes. Nothing ever works out. I am scared, nervous, anxious, alone, and I can't do anything to change it. I wake up feeling depressed, insecure, unsure, unsettled, in my younger years, crying.

I wander around, panicked, looking for the correct classroom, I dread having the teacher lay into me about missing classes.

The feeling is extreme anxiety, embarrassment, and shame.

[I am] completely freaked out that I know nothing and am going to fail the class. The feeling of not knowing and of impending failure is so intensely gut wrenching.

I wake up with my heart pounding every time.

But then, all of a sudden, there even popped up a whole new subject about which I hadn't been informed. But I had to make a written exam about it. I am panicking, I am in agony; all I have studied for, all the hard work was in vain, no degree.

I feel embarrassed in the dream and confused about why I am a bad student, but I also know it to be true and unchangeable. I feel completely unempowered and ashamed.

I am in despair—why did I enroll again in classes I don't need [and will fail]? I am running the halls wondering what to do.

Sick anxiety, sadness, despair, overwhelm—I can NOT possibly succeed here.

I always wake up, soaked with sweat and shaking. It's always a very vivid dream. It's one that I can remember with lots of details long after waking up, unlike most dreams that I have.

The dreams always revolve around me walking around, either high school or college, panicked and on the verge of tears because I can't remember my schedule. . . . I wake up sweating, with my heart pounding, and it takes quite a bit of time for the adrenaline to wear off.

For some, the panic is modulated by the simultaneous awareness, within the dream, that they are, in real life, done with school. Here's an example:

I always have a feeling of dread bordering on panic, but yet at the same time an awareness that I am an adult and it really doesn't matter.

The most common school dream themes are (a) missing classes all term and therefore being likely to fail, and (b) being unable to find the classroom.

My own most common school dream is one in which I suddenly discover, in high school or college, that I have been enrolled in some class that I was unaware of or had forgotten about and never attended. It is the day of the final exam, and I am searching through dungeon-like hallways trying to find the classroom. I finally get to the classroom, late, and I realize that I have no idea what the subject is and can't make heads or tails of the exam questions. I used to think this was an odd dream, probably representing some unique aspect of my personality, but now, in this survey, I have learned that this is the most common of all school dreams, at least among those who responded to the survey.

To conduct the qualitative analysis, I first read all of the dream reports and made notes concerning the themes that seemed to occur frequently. I then reread all of the reports and coded each dream for the presence or absence of each theme that I had previously listed.

The most common theme was that of having missed a course all semester, usually in high school but sometimes in college, and then having to take a final exam in that course. This theme was reported as recurrent by 69 (54 percent) of the respondents. It was often accompanied by feelings of embarrassment and stupidity about missing the course, anxiety or panic about impending failure, and feelings of dread about having to spend another year in school because of this failure.

The second most common theme was that of being lost in school (usually high school), unable to find the right classroom, accompanied by embarrassment, shame, anxiety, or panic about showing up late. This theme was reported by 55 (43 percent) of the respondents.

As in the case of my own recurrent dream, the theme of

not being able to find the class was often combined with the theme of missing the class all semester. A total of 35 respondents (27 percent) reported a recurring dream in which they had missed a course all semester and now, late in the term, typically on final exam day, were searching for the classroom and couldn't find it. Why this dream? On this, your guess is as good as mine.

A variation of the can't-find-the-class dream is the can't-open-my-locker dream. Thirteen respondents reported this theme, typically accompanied by feelings of anxiety or panic about being late for class or unable to attend class because of not being able to get the correct materials or their class schedule out of their locker.

Another common theme is that of having to go back to school as an adult.

The third most common dream theme—after the missed-class-all-semester and can't-find-the-classroom themes—is that of being forced, as an adult, to go back to high school, or even elementary school, because of some bureaucratic snafu or the discovery that the dreamer had failed to meet some requirement. Twenty-one (17 percent) of the survey respondents reported such a recurrent dream. Here are two examples:

In the dream, I'm already a doctor in practice (which I am in real life), but I suddenly realize that I never actually graduated from high school, and I have to go back and finish high school classes. It always happens in the middle of a semester, too, so I know I'm going to be behind, and the teacher is going to wonder where I've been the whole semester. . . . Even while dreaming, I know that I'm already working as a doctor, and it seems crazy that I have to go back and finish something at high school level. When I wake up, I always have the same feeling: "I knew that couldn't be right! I graduated from high school 35 years ago."

I am forced to go back to high school at my current age and relearn all of the material in order to graduate. All of the people with whom I went to high school are still there and are still their same high school age, but I am older, my current age. . . . I feel like a bad student, which is frustrating, because I have a graduate degree! I feel trapped by the pointlessness of the school bureaucracy and the ridiculousness of being made to repeat high school. I contemplate dropping out but simultaneously feel mortified by such a decision.

School anxiety dreams can continue for decades after graduation.

I asked the survey respondents to indicate the number of years that had passed since they had last been a student in the kind of school that was the setting of their recurrent dream. The responses varied from about five years up to about 60 years. On the basis of those responses, I made guesses about the age of each participant and found a range from 20 years up to 77 years old, with most (72 percent) being in their 30s or 40s. Regardless of age, respondents generally indicated that the dream had remained pretty much the same over the years, though some indicated that, with time, it had become less frequent and in some cases less anxiety-provoking.

Here are three examples of reports from respondents in their 60s:

> [Finished high school in 1970.] I have many recurring dreams about school, . . . all of them riddled with anxiety. . . . [In one], I am even back in elementary school. In this variation I am still my grown-up self or at least college age in a classroom of elementary school children. . . . In another . . ., the setting can be high school or college, I have somehow totally forgotten to attend a class for an entire semester and I still have to take the final exam.

> I am over 60 and am so surprised that so many others have the same dream as me. I am in the hall of my high school and cannot find my classroom. It is about a level 5 of stress. Then I doubt myself even further and am unsure of my class schedule. Then my memory fails me even more and I can't remember what days I have a class or if I am still in that class. The dream usually ends there but I sometimes become aware that I already graduated.

> I am 62. I have had frequent dreams of being in middle school walking up stairs, walking down hallways in search of my room. I also have dreams of getting lost trying to get to college, somehow I end up walking through corn fields, prairies, needing to catch a train. Sometimes I make it to

class but if I do then I haven't done my homework, or I missed too many classes.

Well, I'm not Freud or Jung; I don't have a theory about why these particular dreams are so common or what they might mean about the mind's inner workings. How sad, though, that schooling, which is more or less required by law of all young people, produces, as one of its consequences, a lifetime of bad dreams. Hmm. I wonder if it would be possible to devise a way for our children to become educated that would leave them with a lifetime of good dreams, not bad ones. Wouldn't that be something worth striving for? Any ideas how to do that?

It's also interesting to me that many of the respondents indicated that they actually were very good, punctual students, who rarely missed classes and never failed. I wonder if we "good students" actually have worse dreams about school than those "bad students" who sat in the back of the class and shot spitballs.

Reference

Mathes, J., Schrdl, M., & Goritz, A. (2014). Frequency of typical dream themes in most recent dreams: An online study. *Dreaming*, 24, 57-66.

11

What Einstein, Twain, and Forty-Eight Others Said About School

"I was at the foot of my class." –Thomas Edison

JULY 26, 2011

Throughout history, from Plato on, creative people have spoken out against the stultifying effects of compulsory education. Here are quotations from 50 such people, which I have culled partly from my own reading but mostly from various other websites.

Albert Einstein
It is, in fact, nothing short of a miracle that the modern methods of education have not yet entirely strangled the holy curiosity of inquiry; for this delicate plant, aside from stimulation, stands mainly in need of freedom; without this it goes to wrack and ruin without fail. It is a very grave mistake to think that the enjoyment of seeing and searching can be promoted by means of coercion and a sense of duty.

One had to cram all this stuff into one's mind, whether one liked it or not. This coercion had such a deterring effect that, after I had passed the final examination, I found the consideration of any scientific problems distasteful to me for an entire year.

Whoever undertakes to set himself up as a judge of Truth and Knowledge is shipwrecked by the laughter of the Gods.

Plato
Knowledge that is acquired under compulsion obtains no hold on the mind.

Chuang Tzu
Reward and punishment is the lowest form of education.

Mark Twain
I have never let my schooling interfere with my education.

Soap and education are not as sudden as a massacre, but they are more deadly in the long run.

Education consists mainly in what we have unlearned.

In the first place God made idiots. This was for practice. Then he made school boards.

Oscar Wilde
The whole theory of modern education is radically unsound. Fortunately in England, at any rate, education produces no

effect whatsoever. If it did, it would prove a serious danger to the upper classes, and probably lead to acts of violence.

Education is an admirable thing, but it is well to remember from time to time that nothing that is worth knowing can be taught.

Everyone who is incapable of learning has taken to teaching.

Winston Churchill
How I hated schools, and what a life of anxiety I lived there. I counted the hours to the end of every term, when I should return home.

I always like to learn, but I don't always like to be taught.

Woody Allen
I loathed every day and regret every moment I spent in a school.

Dolly Parton
I hated school. Even to this day, when I see a school bus it's just depressing to me. The poor little kids.

George Bernard Shaw
There is nothing on earth intended for innocent people so horrible as a school.

What we call education and culture is for the most part nothing but the substitution of reading for experience, of literature for life, of the obsolete fictitious for the contemporary real.

Finley Peter Dunne
It don't make much difference what you study, so long as you don't like it.

Thomas Edison
I remember that I was never able to get along at school. I was at the foot of the class.

Henry David Thoreau
What does education often do? It makes a straight-cut ditch of a free, meandering brook.

How could youths better learn to live than by at once trying the experiment of living?

Bertrand Russell
Men are born ignorant, not stupid; they are made stupid by education.

Education is one of the chief obstacles to intelligence and freedom of thought.

Benjamin Franklin
He was so learned that he could name a horse in nine languages; so ignorant that he bought a cow to ride on.

H. L. Mencken
The average schoolmaster is and always must be essentially an ass, for how can one imagine an intelligent man engaging in so puerile an avocation.

George Saville, Marquis of Hallifax
The vanity of teaching doth oft tempt a man to forget that he is a blockhead.

Joseph Stalin (Hmmm, a supporter of compulsory schooling.)
Education is a weapon, whose effect depends on who holds it in his hands and at whom it is aimed.

Norman Douglas
Education is a state-controlled manufactory of echoes.

Paul Karl Feyerabend
The best education consists in immunizing people against systematic attempts at education.

Theodore Roosevelt
A man who has never gone to school may steal from a freight car; but if he has a university education, he may steal the whole railroad.

Hector Hugh Munro
But, good gracious, you've got to educate him first. You can't expect a boy to be vicious till he's been to a good school.

Robert Frost
Education is hanging around until you've caught on.

Gilbert K. Chesterton
Education is the period during which you are being
instructed by somebody you do not know, about something
you do not want to know.

Ralph Waldo Emerson
I pay the schoolmaster, but it is the schoolboys who educate
my son.

Alice James
I wonder whether if I had an education I should have been
more or less a fool than I am.

Helen Beatrix Potter
Thank goodness I was never sent to school; it would have
rubbed off some of the originality.

Margaret Mead
My grandmother wanted me to have an education, so she
kept me out of school.

William Hazlitt
Anyone who has passed through the regular gradations
of a classical education, and is not made a fool by it, may
consider himself as having had a very narrow escape.

Laurence J. Peter
Education is a method whereby one acquires a higher grade of prejudices.

Anne Sullivan (I bow to her.)
I am beginning to suspect all elaborate and special systems of education. They seem to me to be built up on the supposition that every child is a kind of idiot who must be taught to think.

Alice Duer Miller
It is among the commonplaces of education that we often first cut off the living root and then try to replace its natural functions by artificial means. Thus we suppress the child's curiosity and then when he lacks a natural interest in learning he is offered special coaching for his scholastic difficulties.

Florence King
Showing up at school already able to read is like showing up at the undertaker's already embalmed: people start worrying about being put out of their jobs.

Emma Goldman
Since every effort in our educational life seems to be directed toward making of the child a being foreign to itself, it must of necessity produce individuals foreign to one another, and in everlasting antagonism with each other.

Edward M. Forster
Spoon feeding in the long run teaches us nothing but the shape of the spoon.

William John Bennett
If [our schools] are still bad maybe we should declare educational bankruptcy, give the people their money and let them educate themselves and start their own schools.

John Updike
School is where you go between when your parents can't take you, and industry can't take you.

Robert Buzzell
The mark of a true MBA is that he is often wrong but seldom in doubt.

Robert M. Hutchins
The three major administrative problems on a campus are sex for the students, athletics for the alumni, and parking for the faculty.

The college graduate is presented with a sheepskin to cover his intellectual nakedness.

Elbert Hubbard
You can lead a boy to college, but you cannot make him think.

Max Leon Forman
Education seems to be in America the only commodity of which the customer tries to get as little as he can for his money.

Phillip K. Dick
The trouble with being educated is that it takes a long time; it uses up the better part of your life and when you are finished what you know is that you would have benefited more by going into banking.

David P. Gardner
Much that passes for education is not education at all but ritual. The fact is that we are being educated when we know it least.

Ivan Illich
The public school has become the established church of secular society.

Together we have come to realize that the right to learn is curtailed by the obligation to attend school.

Marshall McLuhan
The school system . . . is the homogenizing hopper into which we toss our integral tots for processing.

Michel De Montaigne
We only labor to stuff the memory, and leave the conscience and the understanding unfurnished and void.

Peter Drucker
When a subject becomes totally obsolete we make it a required course.

C. C. Colton
Examinations are formidable even to the best prepared, for the greatest fool may ask more than the wisest man can answer.

Paul Simon
When I think back on all the crap I learned in high school, it's a wonder I can think at all.

John Dewey
It is our American habit, if we find the foundations of our educational structure unsatisfactory, to add another story or a wing.

Anonymous (My favorite of all historical figures.)
If nobody dropped out of eighth grade, who would hire the college graduates?

Public school is a place of detention for children placed in the care of teachers who are afraid of the principal, principals who are afraid of the school board, school boards who are afraid of the parents, parents who are afraid of the children, and children who are afraid of nobody.

The creative person is usually rebellious. He or she is the survivor of a trauma called education.

You can always tell a Harvard man, but you can't tell him much.

Yes, I know, this is a biased sampling of quotations! I have deliberately selected quotations that complain about the compulsory, standard system of schooling. But, I challenge you. Develop a list this long of quotations supporting compulsory schooling and see if the authors you quote rank close to these authors in creative genius.

12

When Is Teaching an
Act of Aggression?

*Coercive teaching is always an
act of aggression and can lead
to anger in both directions*

JUNE 3, 2011

Teaching is a word that has something of a halo around it
in our society. We tend to think of it as altruistic. But then
there's this: "I'll teach you a lesson you'll never forget, you
little *^#&@!"

*Not long ago, teaching children was more or less synonymous
with beating them.*

There was a time in our history when teaching children was
pretty much synonymous with beating them. Most of what
the Bible, for example, has to say about teaching children concerns beating. Here are some lines from Proverbs:

"Do not withhold correction from a child, for if you beat him with a rod, he will not die. You shall beat him with a rod and deliver his soul from hell." (Proverbs 22:13-14)

"Foolishness is bound up in the heart of a child, but the rod of correction shall drive it far from him." (Proverbs 22:15)

"Blows that hurt cleanse away evil, as do stripes the inner depths of the heart." (Proverbs 20:30)

"He that spares his rod hates his son, but he that loves him chastens him." (Proverbs 13:24)

My guess is that the Biblical authors understood that children would learn on their own, without teaching, most of the skills and information they needed to know, but wouldn't learn obedience on their own—at least not obedience of the unquestioned, subservient sort that Biblical and societal injunctions of that time demanded. So obedience had to be taught, and punishment was the means for teaching it.

The church-run schools of the 17th, 18th, and 19th centuries, which served as the models for subsequent state-run compulsory schools, were clearly meant to be correctional institutions. They were built on the assumption that children are natural sinners. To save their souls and turn them into good servants, children had to be taught to suppress their willfulness and obey their superiors. The explicitly stated purpose of many of those schools was to beat the fear of God into children, and, as a corollary, to beat into them the fear of teachers, fathers, and other earthly lords and masters. One German schoolmaster proudly kept a record of all the beatings he administered in 51 years of teaching (quoted by Mulhern, 1959): "911,527 blows with a rod, 124,010 blows with a cane, 20,989 taps with a ruler, 136,715 blows with the hand, 10,235 blows to the mouth, 7,905 boxes on the ear, and 1,118,800 blows on the head."

Perhaps that schoolmaster, like the author of Proverbs, would contend that all those beatings were altruistic. Perhaps they were administered purely for the good of the children, not to satisfy a sadistic craving. Perhaps each blow was preceded, quite genuinely, with the statement, "This is going to hurt me more than it hurts you; it's entirely for your good." Hmmm . . .

Even today, obedience is the main lesson of schooling, and punishment is the main vehicle for teaching it.

What about the teaching that goes on in modern schools? Surely we have made progress. Or have we?

The lessons in schools are still mostly about obedience. Children must obey the school rules, which they have no voice in creating, and must obey all of the "requests" (which are really demands) made by their teachers. They must do their assignments, all in accordance with the teachers' precise directions on how and when to do them, whether or not the assignments seem reasonable or worthwhile. The children who get into trouble in school today are still the ones who don't obey. In fact, today's children must spend far greater portions of their lives obeying schoolteachers than did children of any time in the past. We rarely admit it, but teaching in schools today is at least as much about breaking children's wills, and getting them to follow the teachers will, as it was in times past. In fact, if children are too willful in school today we drug them.

Beating is no longer the preferred mode of punishment in schools (though corporal punishment is still permitted in 20 U.S. states). Now the primary tool of school coercion is the grade. Teachers, parents, and society in general drill into children's heads the idea that high grades are essential to success in life. You need at least minimal grades to pass from one level to the next in school and eventually get out of it. You need higher grades to get into college. You need the highest grades to get into any of the "best" colleges; and many kids are made to feel that if they don't get into one of those "best" colleges they will be lifetime failures, disappointments to all who know them. I've known kids who would rather get a beating than a B. The brutality of punishment is in the eye of the punished.

Hmm. . . . Are we really more humane in our methods of schooling now than we were when beatings were the norm? Perhaps we feel better about administering grades than beatings, but do the kids feel better? Our method of punishment in school today seems to create more anxiety, depression, cynicism, and cheating than did the beatings of times past. You got the beating and it was over; but grades and the anxiety they create never end, at least not as long as you are in school. Hey, I'm not for going back to beatings. I'm for chucking out the whole system.

Any coercive teaching is an act of aggression.

Now, to the question posed in the title to this essay: When is teaching an act of aggression? My answer is that any coercive teaching is an act of aggression. Any teaching that that is not wanted by the student, but is forced on the student, is an act of aggression. Any educational use of rewards or punishments to make students learn is an act of aggression.

Why do I say that use of rewards, not just use of punishments, is an act of aggression? Because rewards are rewards only if they can be withheld, and their withholding is not different from punishment. Is a "B" for "good performance" a reward or a punishment? For the student who feels she "desperately needs" an A, it's punishment. A trophy is reward for the one who gets it, but punishment for the one who doesn't. Some psychologists have long argued, quite simplistically, that reward is good and punishment is bad as motivators in teaching, but, in truth, reward and punishment are two sides of the same coin. You can't use one without the other. The carrot is reward for the one who gets it but punishment for the one who doesn't; the stick is punishment for the one who gets it but reward for the one who doesn't.

Let me be clear in stating that I am not against all uses of punishments and rewards. Every society in one way or another punishes people who violate the serious rules of that society. I'm not against punishment for crimes. Even hunter-gatherers, who are so reluctant to use violence, have ways of punishing people who violate the core rules of their society (Gray, 2009). If a hunter-gatherer adult engages in some taboo act—such as trying to boss other people around, or having sex with a first-degree relative or with someone else's spouse, or refusing to share food, or striking a child—the whole social group may, in concert, punish that person. The first round of punishment involves ridicule. The group will talk loudly, in belittling terms, about the person, or they may make up and sing songs designed to shame the person; and the ridicule will continue until the appropriate apologies are made and the behavior is corrected. If ridicule doesn't work, the next step is shunning. People will act as if the offending person no longer exists. That is severe punishment, and it almost always brings the offender around. Either that, or it causes him to leave the band and try his luck with another. Ridicule and shunning are clearly acts of aggression (even if they are not acts of violence), but they are justifiable acts of aggression, aimed at correcting truly antisocial behavior.

What I am against is the use of punishment and rewards as part of teaching children skills and knowledge or teaching them to follow arbitrary rules, rules that have nothing to do with social justice. A child who truly hurts another person or violates some serious social rule may in some cases need to be punished in some way for it. That's entirely different from punishing a child for not reading what the teacher asked the child to read or for not feeling like doing arithmetic today or this year.

Punishment is so fully and intimately woven into the fabric of our schooling system that it's impossible for most people to see how to separate education from punishment. They can be separated only by the radical step of allowing children to take charge of their own education. When that happens, teaching only occurs at the request of the student, and only occurs to the degree that the student wants it. Most people in our society think that can't work; but we know it works for children in hunter-gatherer societies (Gray, 2012); and we know it works for children in our society who attend democratic/free schools or engage in the kind of homeschooling that goes by the name of unschooling (Gray, 2017). Punishment is inevitable when the requirement of your job is to make a child learn something that the child doesn't want to learn. A teacher whose continued employment depends on making her students pass a state-mandated test full of questions that are of no interest to the students has no choice but to use coercive means.

Use of punishment in teaching may make the teacher feel anger toward the student, as well as make the student feel anger toward the teacher.

You might argue, as the author of Proverbs might, that punishing is not an act of aggression if the punisher believes it is a benign act and does not feel aggressive, or angry, while doing it. I suppose you could say, in that case, that it is aggression from the viewpoint of the one being punished but not from that of the one giving the punishment. But here's something to think about. Is it even possible, generally, to administer punishment without feeling anger toward the one being punished?

In my early days as a researcher (I regret to say) I conducted some experiments on learning under conditions of stress, which involved giving moderately painful electric shocks to rats. I convinced myself that giving those shocks, for the purpose of scientific research, was a benign act. But then, as I carried out the experiments, I noticed something strange: My act of shocking those rats made me feel angry toward the rats! When I did experiments with rats that did not involve punishment I generally liked the rats; but when I shocked the poor beasts I felt anger toward them. Anger toward them, not toward me, the person who perhaps deserved the anger. And then, when I began teaching in college, I started to notice the same thing happening. I caught myself sometimes feeling anger toward students who got low grades in my courses. Why? They hadn't done anything to hurt me. And then I began to notice that it wasn't just me. My colleagues also seemed to feel and in various ways express anger toward students to whom they were giving low grades. The low grades came from poor test performances, not from any sort of offensive behavior toward us teachers; so why should they generate anger in us?

There are various ways of explaining this, but my guess is that the anger has at least partly to do with the way we are wired. Punishment and anger are entwined in our nervous systems. Throughout our evolution as primates, we administered punishment primarily if not entirely to those who made us angry. We punished those who hurt us; we punished sexual rivals; we punished those who seemed to be trying to usurp our position in the dominance hierarchy. Something in my nervous system says that if I am punishing those rats or students (with shocks or Ds), then I must be mad at them. If there's no real reason why I should be mad at them, then I must, through some unconscious means, make something up. I'm not saying that this always happens, but it seems to be a pretty strong tendency.

I suspect that this effect—in which low grades engender anger in the grader as well as in the student—occurs more often than most teachers are prepared to admit. I suspect that is part of the reason why teachers burn out. I suspect it is one of the causes of the adversarial relationship that so often occurs between teachers and students. It's not just students being angry at teachers; it's also teachers being angry at students.

Of course, when students ask for feedback and we give them our honest critical opinion, the story is different. That's not punishment and it doesn't generate anger in either direction if the student's request and teacher's criticism are genuine. If our schools were humane, they would be places where students were in charge of their own learning and any help and feedback given by teachers would come at students' requests. There would be no aggression involved.

References

Gray, P. (2009). Play as a foundation for hunter-gatherer social
    existence. *American Journal of Play*, 1, 476-522.
Gray, P. (2012). The value of a play-filled childhood in development
    of the hunter-gatherer individual. In Narvaez, D., Panksepp, J.,

Schore, A., & Gleason, T. (Eds.), *Evolution, Early Experience and Human Development: From Research to Practice and Policy*, pp. 252-370. New York: Oxford University Press, 2012.

Gray, P. (2017). Self-directed education—unschooling and democratic schooling. In G. Noblit (Ed.), *Oxford research encyclopedia of education*. New York: Oxford University Press.

Mulhern, J. (1959). *A history of education: A social interpretation*, 2nd edition.

13

The Danger of Back to School

Children's mental health crises plummet in the summer and rise in the school year

AUGUST 7, 2014

Imagine a job in which your work every day is microman-aged by your boss. You are told exactly what to do, how to do it, and when to do it. You are required to stay in your seat until your boss says you can move. Each piece of your work is evaluated and compared, every day, with the work done by your fellow employees. You are rarely trusted to make your own decisions. Research on employment shows that this is not only the most tedious employment situation, but also the most stressful. Micromanagement drives people crazy.

Kids are people, and they respond just as adults do to mi-cromanagement, to severe restrictions on their freedom, and to constant, unsolicited evaluation. School, too often, is ex-actly like the kind of nightmare job that I just described; and, worse, it is a job that kids are not allowed to quit. No matter how much they might be suffering, they are forced to continue, unless they have enlightened parents who have the means, know-how, and will to get them out of it. Including homework, the hours are often more than those that their parents put into their full-time jobs, and freedom of movement for children at school is far less than that for their parents at work.

In the late 19th and early 20th centuries, many people became concerned about the ill effects of child labor on children's wellbeing and development, and laws were passed to ban it. But now we have school, expanded to such a degree that it is equivalent to a full-time job—a psychologically stressful, sedentary full-time job, for which the child is not paid and does not gain the sense of independence and pride that can come from a real job.

Elsewhere (Gray, 2011, 2013) I have presented evidence that children, especially teenagers, are less happy in school than in any other setting where they regularly find themselves and that increased schooling, coupled with decreased freedom outside of school, correlates, over decades, with sharply increased rates of psychiatric disorders in young people, including major depression and anxiety disorders.

Now, in August, we are beginning to see the "back to school" ads, and I have been wondering about the relationship of children's mental health to the school year. It occurred to me that an index of that relationship might be the numbers of psychiatric emergency room visits by school-age children that occur each month. Do they decrease in the summer, when (for most kids) school is not in session?

In a rather extensive search of the published literature, I found only one publicly available set of data on this—in an online article dealing with children's emergency psychiatric visits at Connecticut Children's Mental Center in Hartford (Becker, 2014). The primary point of the article was that such visits have risen dramatically in recent years and wait times in the ER have grown longer. However, an interactive graph in the article shows the number of such emergency visits for every month, for every year from 2000 through 2013. Even a quick glance at the graph made it obvious that, every year, the number of visits dropped in the summer and rose again in the school year.

In order to quantify this, I calculated the average number of visits, per calendar month, for three years—2011 through 2013. I included only those visits that were serious enough to lead to at least one overnight stay at the center (including all visits would have produced the same general finding). Here are the data:

Average Number of Emergency Psychiatric Visits at Connecticut Children's Mental Center in Hartford

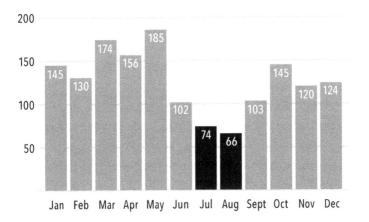

Just as I predicted, July and August are the months with, by far, the fewest children's psychiatric ER visits. In fact, the average number of visits for those two months combined (70 per month) is less than half of the average during the full school months (142 visits per month for the nine months excluding June, July, and August). June, which has some school days (a number that varies depending on the number of snow days to be made up), is also low, but not as low as July and August. Interestingly, and not predicted by my hypothesis, September is also relatively low, equivalent to June. It seems plausible that September is a relatively relaxed warm-up month in school; serious tests, heavy assignments, and report cards are yet to come. It may take a few weeks back in school before the stress really kicks in.

Someone might argue that the seasonal variation in mental health crises reflects the weather, not the school year. However, that argument falls on its face when we look at the other months. The month with the highest rate of children's mental health ER visits is May, and May is generally a beautiful month, weather-wise, in Connecticut, but it may well be the toughest month of school. May is the month of final tests, due dates for papers, and the crunch to make it through the rest of the curriculum.

These, admittedly, are data from just one children's mental health center. I'd love to find more data to test the hypothesis. [Note added in preparing this collection: I have since found more data, available in the next essay.] Meanwhile, if you are a parent of a school-age child thinking about "back to school," keep this in mind: The available evidence suggests quite strongly that school is bad for children's mental health. Of course, it's bad for their physical health, too; nature did not design children to be cooped up all day at a micromanaged, sedentary job.

References

Becker, A. L. (2014). Children stuck in crisis: Connecticut's psychiatric emergency gets worse. *The CT Mirror*, July 10, 2014. Downloaded at https://ctmirror.org/2014/07/10/a-crisis-gets-worse-connecticut-childrens-psychiatric-emergency/

Gray, P. (2011). The decline of play and the rise of psychopathology in childhood and adolescence. *American Journal of Play*, 3, 443-463.

Gray, P. (2013). *Free to Learn: Why Unleashing the Instinct to Play Will Make Our Children Happier, More Self-Reliant, and Better Students for Life*. Basic Books.

14

Children's and Teens' Suicides Related to the School Calendar

Psychiatric emergencies and youth suicides rise sharply with the school year.

MAY 31, 2018

We get very upset by school shootings, as well we should. Every such instance is a national tragedy. But as serious as this tragedy is, it is dwarfed by another school-related tragedy—suicide. Suicide is the third leading cause of death for school-aged children over 10 years old and the second leading cause (behind accidents and ahead of homicides) for those over 15 (Vanorman & Jarosz, 2016). The evidence is now overwhelming that our coercive system of schooling plays a large role in these deaths and in the mental anguish so many young people experience below the threshold of suicide.

Four years ago I presented data—from a mental health facility in Connecticut—showing the relationship between pediatric emergency mental health visits and the school year over a three-year period (2011-2013). [See the previous essay in this collection.] Those data revealed that the average monthly number of emergency mental health intakes for school-aged children declined from 185 in May (the last full month of school), to 102 in June (the month in which school lets out), and then down to 74 and 66, respectively, in July and August (the full months of freedom from school). In September the rate started its climb back up again. Overall, the rate of such visits during the school months was slightly more than twice what it was in July and August. When I wrote that article, I could not find other studies assessing mental health breakdowns as a function of the school calendar. Since that time, more research has emerged.

Psychiatric Breakdowns and Suicide Attempts as a Function of the School Year

Collin Lueck and his colleagues (2015) examined the rate of psychiatric visits for danger to self or others at a large pediatric emergency mental health department in Los Angeles on a week-by-week basis for the years 2009-2012. They found that the rate of such visits in weeks when school was in session was 118 percent greater than in weeks when school wasn't in session In other words, the rate of emergency psychiatric visits was more than twice as high during school weeks as it was during non-school weeks. It's interesting to note that the sharp decline in such emergencies occurred not just during summer vacation, but also during school vacation weeks over the rest of the year.

The researchers also found a continuous increase in the average rate of psychiatric emergencies during school weeks, but not during vacation weeks, over the four-year period of the study. This result supports the hypothesis that the increase in such emergencies over the four-year period was the result of the increased stressfulness of school over that time period and not attributable to some factor independent of schooling. In another, more recent study, Gregory Plemmons and his colleagues (2018) found that the rate of hospitalization of school-aged children for suicidal ideation and attempts increased dramatically—by nearly 300 percent—over the seven years of their study, from 2008 to 2015, and each year the rate of such hospitalizations was significantly higher in the school months than in the summer.

Actual Suicides as a Function of the School Year

On the basis of the data I've described so far, someone could argue that the school-year increase in emergency psychiatric admissions is a result of attentive behavior on the part of school personnel, who referred children for admissions and thereby, perhaps, saved children's lives. According to that view, parents are less perceptive of children's problems than are teachers. There are no data suggesting that this is true, however, and there are very strong reasons to believe it is not true. If this hypothesis were true, then the rate of actual suicides—as opposed to suicide ideation or attempts—should be lower when school is in session than when it is not. But, in

fact, the actual suicide data parallel the data for suicide ideation and attempts.

Benjamin Hansen and Matthew Lang (2011) used data
collected from state agencies to analyze suicides for teenagers
across the U.S. between 1980 and 2004. This is an older study,
with data largely from a time when school was at least somewhat less stressful than it is today and the total teen suicide
rate was lower than today. Yet, they found a much higher rate
of suicides during the school year than during the summer
vacation months. They also—unlike any of the other studies
I've found—analyzed the data separately for boys and girls.
For boys, the suicide rate was, on average, 95 percent higher
during the school months than during summer vacation; for
girls, it was 33 percent higher. This finding is consistent with
the general observation that boys have a more difficult time
adjusting to the constraints of school than do girls. Stated differently, when girls commit suicide, school is apparently less
likely to be a cause than is the case for boys.

Hansen and Lang also found that the school-year increase in teen suicide rates held only for those of school
age. For 18-year-olds, most of whom would be finished with
high school, the increase was barely present, and for 19- and
20-year-olds it had vanished. Other research shows that suicides and suicide attempts for adults vary only slightly by
season and are somewhat higher, not lower, in the summer
than in the fall and winter (Miller et al, 2012; Cambria et al,
2016)—a trend that is opposite to the finding for school-aged
children and teens.

Just the Tip of the Iceberg

Actual suicides and emergency mental health admissions are just the tip of the iceberg of the distress that school produces in young people. I summarize some of the other indicators of that stress in the next essay. One finding that bears repeating comes from a large survey conducted a few years ago by the American Psychological Association, which revealed that teenagers are the most stressed, anxious people in America; that 83 percent of them cite school as a cause of their stress; and that, during the school year, 27 percent of them reported experiencing "extreme stress" compared to 13 percent reporting that during the summer.

School is clearly bad for children's mental health. The tragedy is that we continue to make school ever more stressful, even though research shows that none of this is necessary. Young people learn far more, far better, with much less stress (and at less public expense) when they are allowed to learn in their own natural ways, as I have pointed out in many of my other articles and in my book, *Free to Learn*.

References

Cambria, D. G., et al (2016). Do suicide attempts occur more frequently in the spring too? A systematic review and rhythmic analysis. *Journal of Affective Disorders*, 196, 125-137.

Hansen, B. & Lang, M. (2011). Back to school blues: Seasonality of youth suicide and the academic calendar. *Economics of Education Review*, 30, 850-851.

Lueck, C., et al (2015). Do emergency pediatric psychiatric visits for danger to self or others correspond to times of school attendance? *American Journal of Emergency Medicine*, 33, 682-684.

Miller, T. R., et al (2012). Suicide deaths and nonfatal hospital admissions for deliberate self-harm in the United Sates. *Crisis*, 33, 169-177.

Plemmons, G., et al (2018). Hospitalization for suicide ideation or attempt: 2008-2015. *Pediatrics*, 141 #6.

Vanorman, A., & Jarosz, B. (2016). Suicide replaces homicide as second-leading cause of death among U.S. teenagers. Website of Population Reference Bureau (PRB). Downloaded at https://www.prb.org/suicide-replaces-homicide-second-leading-cause-death-among-us-teens/

15

What If Medicine's First Principle Were Also Education's?

What if state-sponsored schools had to prove that they do more good than harm?

SEPTEMBER 10, 2016

Primum non nocere. First, do no harm. As part of becoming a doctor, students at most medical colleges must take an oath, derived partly from the ancient Hippocratic oath, in which they declare their understanding that the first principle of medical practice is "do no harm." Of course, many medical treatments do, necessarily, entail some harm; so what this principle means in practice is that any potential harm to a patient must be balanced against the projected benefit for that patient, and there must be good evidence that the benefit will outweigh the harm.

What if our compulsory schooling system had to provide evidence, for every child, that the benefit of its schooling outweighs the harm? Here's little Suzy, 5 years old. The state says she has to start kindergarten; neither she nor her parents have any say in the matter (unless the parents are in a position to homeschool or afford some other means of meeting the state's compulsory education requirement). What if the state were required, before they enrolled little Suzy, to prove that the institution they are forcing her into will, in all probability, benefit her more than it hurts her?

If the state had to do this—if they had to live up to a "do no harm" pledge—schooling as we know it would collapse. We would have a sudden, long-overdue educational revolution. In fact, even if the requirement were the less demanding one of proving that the schooling we provide benefits the average child, or most children, more than it hurts them, the system would collapse.

Compulsory schooling is an enormous intrusion into the lives of children and families, and its harm is well documented.
I've sometimes heard from defenders of forced schooling what I refer to as the "bad-tasting medicine" justification. Schooling, they say, may not be pleasant, but it is necessary for the person's long-term wellbeing. Never mind that most medicines take a couple of seconds to swallow while compulsory schooling takes 11 years (or 13 in some states). Never mind that there is no evidence at all that forced schooling does more good for children than can be accomplished with a much more pleasant tasting and less expensive placebo. The placebo I have in mind is unschooling, or democratic/free schooling, where children remain in charge of their own lives and learning, with help when they want it, not coercion, from caring adults.

If schooling were a drug, it would never make it past the

FDA. There is no evidence that it creates more benefits than the placebos I mentioned, and there is a lot of evidence that it inflicts serious damage. Here is just some of that documented evidence:

- A large-scale study involving hundreds of students from many school districts, using an experience sampling method, revealed that students were less happy in school than in any other setting in which they regularly found themselves (Csikszentmihalyi & Hunter, 2003).

- Verbal abuse from teachers is a common occurrence. In one survey, for example, 64 percent of middle school students reported experiencing stress symptoms because of verbal abuse from teachers (Hyman & Perone, 1998). Another study revealed that nearly 30 percent of boys were verbally abused by teachers in kindergarten, and the abuse increased in years after that (Brengden et al., 2006). Surveys of adults indicate that between 50 percent and 60 percent of them recall school-related experiences that, in their view, were psychologically traumatic (McEachern et al., 2008).

- In a study in which 150 college students were asked to described the two most negative experiences in their lives—experiences that negatively affected their development—by far the most frequent category of reports (28 percent of the total) were of traumatic interactions with school teachers (Branan, 1972). In a study in which adults were interviewed to find out about positive, peak learning experiences occurring in their schooling, few could recall such experiences, but many recalled negative experiences, which interfered with rather than supported their development (Olson, 2009).

- Hair cortisol levels in young children were found to be significantly higher in samples taken two months after starting elementary school than in samples taken two months prior to starting elementary school (Groeneveld et al, 2013). Hair cortisol level is reflective of chronic stress, the sort of stress that can seriously impair physical growth and health.

- A large-scale national survey conducted by the American Psychological Association (2014) revealed that U.S. teenagers feel more stressed than do adults and that school is by far the main cause of their stress (noted by 83 percent of the sample). In the same study, 27 percent of teens reported experiencing "extreme stress" during the school year, compared to 13 percent reporting that during the summer.

- The rates of emergency mental health visits and suicides for children and teens are roughly twice as high during school months compared to summer vacation months (see the previous two essays).

To this add the sheer amount of children's and teenagers' time that is wasted by the school system. If you don't believe it ask the principal of your local school for permission to "shadow" a student for a day—that is, spend the whole school day doing just what the student is required to do. The adults I know who have done that—all of whom were teachers—were shocked at the tedium, the time wasted, during which they were not free to occupy themselves with anything of their own choosing. None of them wanted to do it for a second day. Children and teens have no more tolerance for tedium than do adults; they just have no choice in the matter.

Noninvasive education as the alternative to forced schooling

Whenever possible, enlightened, conscientious physicians look for noninvasive or minimally invasive methods to correct medical problems instead of highly invasive methods, such as surgery or toxins, which interfere with the body's integrity and can cause pain, disablement, or even death. Forced schooling is an extraordinarily invasive educational practice. The noninvasive alternative is Self-Directed Education, as in unschooling or democratic free/schooling. Research conducted to date suggests that these modes of education are at least as effective as forced schooling in preparing young people for adult life and far less disruptive of children's and families' day-to-day existence (for a reviews of the evidence, see Gray, 2016, 2017).

But the educational establishment doesn't want to know about that evidence. Those who profit from forced, intrusive education are like surgeons who profit from surgery and don't want to know that there are cheaper, less invasive ways of solving the particular medical problem they have been treating. On the basis of my experiences attempting to get grants to compare directly the consequences of Self-Directed Education with coercive schooling, in well-designed studies, I have concluded that the educational establishment simply does not want anyone to ask the big question: Is our current, compulsory, top-down system of education actually more effective in producing competent, productive, well-employed, happy adults than is noninvasive, Self-Directed Education?

Imagine what would happen if educational foundations actually funded such a comparative study and the results came out showing, in a way that was hard to dispute, that the noninvasive procedure works at least as well as the invasive one by all reasonable measures. How could we then justify the educational behemoth that supports so many careers and enriches so many companies? There would no longer be a need for university departments of education. The need for teachers would be greatly reduced—down to a small number who would be sought out by self-directed learners because of their skills and knowledge, not because of "teaching credentials." There would be little need for textbooks; and, without forced consumers of such books, the prices on them would have to drop and their quality would have to increase.

The revolution in education will come, but it will not come from within the educational establishment. It will come because more and more people are using whatever legal means they can to remove their kids from the invasive system. As this happens, over time, an ever greater number of people will know people who have grown up outside of forced schooling and will see that noninvasive education works. At some point, the floodgates will open, and the educational establishment will become irrelevant, eventually extinct. I hope that point comes while I'm still alive. Please help make it happen.

References

American Psychiatric Association (2014). Stress in America: Are teens adopting adults' stress habits? Downloaded at https://www.apa.org/news/press/releases/stress/2013/stress-report.pdf

Branan, J. M. (1972). Negative human interactions. *Journal of Counseling Psychology*, 19, 81-82.

Brengden, M., Wanner, B., & Vitaro, F. (2006). Verbal abuse by the teacher and child adjustment from kindergarten through grade 6. *Pediatrics*, 117, 1585-1598.

Csíkszentmihályi, M., & Hunter, J. (2003). Happiness in everyday life: The uses of experience sampling. *Journal of Happiness Studies*, 4, 185–199.

Gray, P. (2017). Children's natural ways of learning still work—even for the three Rs. In D. C. Geary & D. B. Berch (Eds), *Evolutionary perspectives on child development and education* (pp. 63-93). Springer.

Gray, P. (2017). Self-directed education—unschooling and democratic schooling. In G. Noblit (Ed.), *Oxford research encyclopedia of education*. New York: Oxford University Press. 2017.

Groeneveld, M. G., et al (2013). Children's hair cortisol as a biomarker of stress at school entry. *Stress: The International Journal on the Biology of Stress*, 16, 711-715.

Hyman, I. A., & Perone, D. C. (1998). The other side of student violence: educator policies and practices that may contribute to student misbehavior. *Journal of School Psychology*, 36, 7-27.

McEachern, A. G., Aluede, O., & Kenny, M. C. (2008). Emotional abuse in the classroom: Implications and interventions for counselors. *Journal of Counseling and Development* 86, 3-10.

Olson, K. *Wounded by School*. Teachers' College Press, 2009.

16

Kindergarten Teachers Are Quitting, and Here Is Why

Comments from exasperated kindergarten teachers throughout the country

DECEMBER 20, 2019

A month ago, I posted an article in my *Psychology Today* blog describing the stand that kindergarten teachers in Brookline, Massachusetts, took in protesting the policies imposed upon them from above—the excessive testing, dreary drill, and lack of opportunity for playful, creative, joyful activities (Gray, 2019). The post went somewhat viral, quickly receiving over 200,000 views and more than 80 comments. Most of the comments were in support of the protesting teachers, and many added further confirmation that the child abuse occurring in Brookline kindergartens is occurring in kindergartens throughout the country.

The abuse is occurring not because kindergarten teachers are mean. Most of them are kindhearted people who love children; that's why they chose the career that they did (though this may change over time as the loving ones quit). The abuse is occurring because the teachers are not being allowed to do what they believe and know is right. They are being required to follow policies imposed from above by people who know little about children and don't have to see the anger, anxiety, and tears that the teachers see in the classrooms. If teachers are at fault, they are so primarily for lack of courage to resist the outrageous demands imposed on them and on the children in their classrooms.

In recent years, I've heard from many elementary school teachers who are quitting, or taking early retirement, because they are no longer willing to take part in an educational system that is harming children. I heard from a new set of them in the comments section of that post describing the Brookline protest. Here, below, are quotations from 16 of those comments. The first 14 are all from different kindergarten teachers, and the final two are from teachers of later grades, who describe the debilitating effects on children as they go beyond kindergarten.

Read them, weep, and then ask yourself what you can do to help remedy this damage created by politicians and narrow-minded educational policymakers who look at numbers and not children.

"I had to retire in 2017 because I could not take the pressure of having to force my 5- and 6-year-old students to sit with books. . . no talking allowed. . . .. I taught for 18 years and in the last 3 years teaching this stuff to my sweet little kinders

I heard students cry, talk about how they didn't understand, say they hated reading time, and act out. We were basically regurgitating the curriculum script. It was awful. I hated going to work that last 2 years with all the stress of academic achievement expectations. . . All administrators want to hear is the exact same stuff from one room to another from school to school.

"Teachers have been complaining about more testing every year. And every year we hear, 'We'll look into that,' and every year someone higher up decides, 'We need more data.' That, in turn, means more testing, more seatwork, and less play. I personally couldn't take it anymore and took early retirement."

"I worked part-time as an art teacher in a kindergarten class. The kindergarten teacher was a drill sergeant, moving the kids from one activity to the next in 15-minute segments. This was covering math, reading, printing letters, etc. Those kids were mostly wound up, usually not settling down. I eventually quit, because I couldn't stand to be around that barking teacher; I can only imagine how the kids felt.

"I have taught kindergarten for nearly 40 years. Common Core expectations for kindergarten seem to have trickled down from the top, and the people who wrote it thought that they could legislate quicker child development. . . . Kindergartners are expected to write sentences and stories, have math discourse, and take tests on the computer. Many of them can't even cross the midline and write an X yet. . . Schools are being driven by 'data'; and kindergarten teachers are being asked to reduce their students to numbers. Please, let's allow them to play!!"

"I taught kindergarten for the last 18 years of my 35-year career. My classroom was play-centered and I think filled with very happy children. I retired 13 years ago, and I'm appalled when I speak to friends who are still teaching. Especially in kindergarten, but throughout school classrooms, there is much too much pressure put on children. . . Play and unstructured time allow children the chance to explore and find their path in the world."

"I've taught kindergarten for 25 years and I can tell you that this article is spot on. Last week I gave my 5-year-olds a reading assessment that required them to infer the meaning of 'bifocals' after hearing a 5-paragraph story about Ben Franklin (the story had no pictures). This is the kind of madness that permeates curriculum design for kindergarten. I'm retiring earlier than I had planned because I just can't be a part of this any longer."

"This heartbroken kindergarten teacher just couldn't teach 'firstergarten' anymore and retired early. I go back to help my teacher buddies who are still being forced to torture children every day with developmentally inappropriate schedules, expectations, and curriculum."

"I wanted to be a developmental K teacher, but by the time I received my credential, things went from bad to worse in K classrooms across America. I foolishly thought I could sneak art and play in, but I was wrong. The Curriculum Cops showed up in the class I was doing my student teaching in, and that was the beginning of the end for me. Now I just sub and sneak in fun for the kids whenever I can. Teaching is dull, dry, and stressful when you have to force small children to do what they are not ready to do. . . The powers that be are getting away with this because teachers (myself included) don't do anything except complain. When are we going to stand up and say, 'Enough is enough'?"

"As a retired early childhood teacher and administrator, I am saddened by the focus and evaluative assessments used to measure growth embedded in public education at this time. Our state mandates assessment that is strictly academic for pre-K and K. Those scores are then 50 percent of the teacher evaluation. If you want to keep your job, you must place focus on academic learning instead of kinesthetic, developmentally appropriate brain, social, and emotional growth."

"I have been a teacher's aide for 15 years. . . We are asking these 5- and 6-year-olds to do things that they are not emotionally able to do, and we are now seeing many young children with anxiety."

"Words that have come out of my mouth this fall: 'We do NOT play in kindergarten. Do not do that again!' (to a student building a very cool 3D scorpion with the math blocks instead of completing his assigned task to practice addition.) 'No, I cannot read Pete the Cat to you. We have to do our reading' (90 minutes of a scripted daily lesson). 'Those clips (hanging from the ceiling) are for when we do art. No, we cannot do any art. We have to do our reading lesson' (my kinders get to go to a 40-minute art class once a month). 'No, you cannot look at the books/play with the toys' (literacy toys and games). 'No, we cannot do a science experiment. We have to do our reading.' 'No, we cannot color. We have to do our reading.» . . . I hate my job. Love my kids—hate the curriculum. But I cannot afford to quit. Too close to retirement to start over."

"I've been teaching kindergarten for thirteen years. In my first year, kids were expected to read at A or B level by the end of the year. That's a book that follows a pattern and changes one word and only requires the kid to show some reading behaviors and phonemic awareness. . . Now it's D level. Those books include multiple lines of text on one page and do not follow a pattern. They include long vowels and digraphs. Kids have to know all 42 phonemic sounds and their variations in spelling, as well as numerous sight words that don't follow phonics rules. Sure, some kids rise to the challenge. Their brains are ready and they're eager to learn. Most, however, don't. . .Pushing them to read causes stress. I've seen a rise in anxiety in my kids, avoidance of tasks that are 'too hard,' and some pretty impressive breakdowns or meltdowns. I've also seen a drop in executive function, imagination, and ability to sit and focus. . .. I have to give them about 13 different required formal tests throughout the year. Thirteen! I'm seeing assessment fatigue. Who knew five- and six-year-olds could burn out? They certainly can, and I worry about how they'll continue through school for the 12 years after I have them."

"Kindergarten should be a transition—with plenty of play and student-centered learning—from nursery to first-grade academic curriculum, but instead children are forgoing that transition. They are being thrown into a structured environment that is requiring them to be mini robots. They have to sit for extended periods of time (even adults find that hard), they have to use 'brain' power without the aid of free movement to stave off boredom. They are not required to use their imaginations or ask questions that stimulate interaction with teachers and peers. . . . Kindergarten classrooms shouldn't have desks and chairs; they should have centers, reading nooks, educational and fun games, and space to explore."

"I was horrified as a teacher as each school year brought new demands on our five-year-olds. Many of these children were not in preschool, so kindergarten was their first exposure to education. We were required to test them immediately for letter sounds, rhyming, counting, shapes, name writing, adding, and of course words. I was sickened by our practice. A few of the kindergarten teachers tried to fight the system. We presented common sense ideas for play and social skills. This was not embraced by our administration leaders. After many years in kindergarten, I chose to move to second grade. I can tell you the children are socially awkward as well as burnt out by 7 and 8. What the heck are we doing to our children? We are creating a society that will hate to be educated and have serious anxiety and social skill issues."

"I teach second grade. I see an ever-increasing gap in social-emotional skills and basics such as pencil grip and penmanship. Outbursts and attitudes of failure enter my room. My mission is to repair that, and then do my best to help them find time to find their passions and talents. The 'must do' rigor, drill and kill, and workbooks for all subjects without integration do not let me apply my talent to the craft of education."

"I have never been a Kindergarten teacher, but I have taught fourth- to eighth-grade students for 37 years. . . In 2006, I left the classroom to serve the school district in another capacity . . . I returned to the district as a substitute in 2015. When I subbed at the school where I had taught from 1997 to 2006, I was shocked to see the misery of the students. They now walked the hallways looking down at their feet. No more smiles, no more laughter from the classrooms. In 2017, I was asked to take over as a long-term sub for a 6th grade teacher who retired . . . I had to use the lesson plans given to me . . . Students were supposed to read silently and answer questions about their reading every day . . . I spoke to the principal and the assistant principal about my concern that the students were not really learning and was told that instruction had to be done this way so students could cover the material they needed to cover to be ready for tests they had to take every three weeks. The students hated the tests, and so did I . . . Twelve-year-old students were expected to use a computer to take several parts of a timed test for up to three hours and 45 minutes per day . . . After I finished my five-month term in this position, I resigned from the school district because I no longer wanted any part of this type of education that I felt was detrimental to the wellbeing of young children."

Wow. Did any of the commenters talk about schools they liked? Yes, four did, but none of those four were teaching in public or conventional private schools in the United States. Two, who talked about lots of play and happy kids, were teaching in Australia; another was teaching in a forest school; the fourth was involved in an early childhood center designed for play and Self-Directed Education outside of the public-school system. And then there was a mom who wrote: "My kids are 6, 4, and 2, and we left our well-ranked Boston suburban school district to move overseas. This was honestly one of the top 5 reasons we left the U.S. My kids are now in a play-based school with no national testing. It's heaven, and we're extremely lucky to have this option open to us."

Reference

Gray, P. (Nov. 12, 2019). Kindergarten teachers speak out for children's happiness. *Psychology Today*, Freedom to Learn blog. Downloaded at https://www.psychologytoday.com/us/blog/ freedom-learn/201911/kindergarten-teachers-speak-out -children-s-happiness

17

Head Start's Value Lies in Care, Not Academic Training

Here's my theory about why some early childhood programs help and others hurt.

FEBRUARY 3, 2020

Head Start was founded in 1965 as part of President Lyndon Johnson's War on Poverty and it has been going strong ever since. This past year the program enrolled about 1 million children nationwide, at a cost of about $10 billion. Does Head Start do what it is supposed to do—give children from poor families a boost that ultimately helps them rise out of poverty? The results of research to address that question are mixed, and here I address the question of why that is so. But first, as prelude, I describe briefly the results of research on two other pre-kindergarten programs aimed at ameliorating the effects of poverty—one that failed and one that succeeded.

The Tennessee Pre-Kindergarten Failure

A few years ago, Tennessee instituted a state-wide pre-kindergarten program for low-income children, and researchers at Vanderbilt University conducted a well-designed research study to determine its effects. Since there were more applicants for the program than there were places, a random process was used to determine who would be admitted and who would not. The researchers subsequently used data from pre-k through third grade, from state educational records, to compare those who were in the program with otherwise similar children who were not.

Here is a summary of the results (from Lipsey et al., 2018). At the end of the pre-k year, those in pre-k performed better than the control group on a set of achievement tests, but during kindergarten and thereafter the children in the control group caught up and surpassed them. On the third-grade state achievement tests, those in the control group performed significantly better than those in the pre-k group in math and science and equally well in reading. Moreover, those in the pre-k group were more likely to be diagnosed as having learning disorders than those in the control group and also had a higher rate of school rule violations.

So, this expensive, intensive program designed to help poor children get a head start in school backfired. The children who, by random selection, were not in the pre-k program performed better academically and behaviorally and were less likely to need special services in elementary school than those who were in the program. Why did the program fail?

My theory is that it failed because it focused too much on academic training and not enough on the real needs of little children. By now there is lots of evidence that early academic training backfires (Gray, 2105a&b). It produces short-term gains, but those gains are illusory; they have to do with memorized procedures that help out on immediate tests but ultimately interfere with the kind of intellectual development needed to achieve later on in school. Unfortunately, education policy makers continue to ignore that evidence.

The researchers' published article on this study did not provide a description of the program, but I found this description of it elsewhere (Strait Talk, 2018): "The program provides a minimum of 5.5 hours of instructional time per day, five days per week. Classes have a maximum of 20 students and are taught by state-licensed teachers using one of 22 curricula approved by the Tennessee Department of Education."

Wow, my heart goes out to those kids! A minimum of 5.5 hours of instruction per day, five days a week, from state-licensed teachers, using a state-determined curriculum, for four-year-olds! It sounds like torture to me. It sounds like a perfect program for making kids hate school even before they start, a perfect program for producing learning disorders in initially normal children. Children are designed to learn, with joy, through self-directed exploration and play. That's how they acquire the basic understandings and intellectual skills that help them with schoolwork and, more important, all of life as they grow older. It looks like this program deprived these kids of what they needed and gave them what they didn't need. They were better off at home.

The Opportunity Project Success

Now here's another well-studied early childhood program, with rosier results. The Opportunity Project, offered to preschool-aged children from economically needy families in a midwestern city, is modeled on guidelines developed by the National Association for the Education of Young Children (NAEYC), carried out according to the following directives (quoted from Bakken et al., 2017): First, learning about diversity is integrated and developmentally appropriate and part of all aspects of the daily schedule. Second, the climate and tone of the classroom reflects a sense of community, where all members are respected for their individuality. Third, classrooms have resources and materials in all areas to make the environment culturally rich (e.g., books about sharing, caring, respect, and differences/similarities among people). Fourth, in the area of self-concept/autonomy, children learn a sense of self, a sense of belonging, and positive attitudes toward learning itself. Fifth, children are encouraged to become active learners, drawing on direct physical and social experiences to construct their understanding of the world around them. And last, learning new skills is based on the interaction of the children's biological maturation and the environment—opportunity is encouraged in learning new skills."

So, this apparently is a program oriented toward the whole child that provides a happy, respectful place for children to interact with one another and adults. To me, it is no surprise that research on this program showed positive results. Assessments in fourth grade revealed that the children from this program scored higher on math and reading tests, had fewer discipline referrals, were significantly more emotionally mature, and were better at social interactions than those who had not been in the program.

Findings such as these fit well with much other research showing that children in traditional play-based preschools and kindergartens perform better—socially, emotionally, and academically—by third or fourth grade than children in academically focused preschools and kindergartens (Gray, 2105a).

The Head Start Program

Now, back to Head Start. As I noted earlier, Head Start was founded in 1965 as part of President Johnson's War on Poverty. This was long before we became obsessed with test scores and academic training for little children—long before No Child Left Behind or Common Core or any of those initiatives that have proven so harmful. Today Head Start is thought of primarily as an early education program, but it was designed to be much more than that. As initially conceived the program had six components, of which education was just one. The other five were (according to Ludwig & Miller, 2007):

- *Parent involvement.* In the first year of the program 47,000 parents from poor families were employed in Head Start centers, and another 500,000 were part-time volunteers (Zigler & Valentine, 1979).

- *Nutrition.* The program provides a nutritious breakfast, lunch, and snacks. Early research showed that Head Start greatly reduced incidences of malnutrition (Fosburg et al., 1984).

- *Social services.* Head Start social workers help families solve some of the crises that come with poverty and connect families with social services to which they are entitled.

- *Mental health services.* Head Start workers help to identify mental health problems among the children and find help to treat them.

- *Health services.* The program provides children with basic health services, including immunizations and screening for such conditions as anemia and diabetes, and connects families with community health centers.

The actual implementation of these aspects of Head Start vary considerably—often in undocumented ways—from place to place and over time.

Mixed Findings Concerning the Success of Head Start

Many research studies have been conducted on the question of whether Head Start truly helps children rise out of poverty. The results have been mixed, but several reviews of the studies have revealed some revealing patterns to the results.

Studies that looked at academic gains in elementary school have produced little evidence of such gains (Piper. 2018, 2019). In contrast, studies that have looked long-term, at the life course of the people who were children in Head Start at or shortly after its inception, have shown quite remarkable gains (Deming, 2009; Bailey et al., 2018). Compared to control groups, those who were in Head Start were found to be significantly less likely to die in childhood (Ludwig & Miller, 2007), less likely to suffer from health problems (Fosberg et al, 1984), more likely to finish high school and go on to college (Bailey et al., 2018), and to be better off socially, emotionally, and economically in adulthood (Deming, 2009; Schanzenbach & Bauer, 2016). These studies are powerful evidence that, at least for the early recruits into the program, Head Start was successful in achieving what it set out to achieve, that is, help people rise out of poverty.

A subsequent study (Pages et al., 2019), however, that looked at the life outcomes of those who were children in Head Start in the 1990s—years after it was initiated—failed to replicate these positive findings. This study, which was conducted by methods identical to those of the study of earlier recruits, revealed no positive gains in childhood or early adulthood for those who had been in Head Start compared to those who had been cared for at home, and on some measures they were doing worse. Those who had been in Head Start were significantly less likely to be employed or in school as young adults.

Why has the Benefit of Head Start Declined Over Time?

Why these different findings? There are many possibilities, but the one that comes to my mind, based on other research, is that the nature of the Head Start program may have changed over the years. I don't know of direct evidence for this, but my hypothesis is that in more recent times Head Start has been affected by the national obsession with academic training, so more such training is going on in the program at the expense of some of the other benefits that the program has traditionally offered.

One reviewer of research on Head Start (Piper, 2018; 2019) has suggested that the greatest benefit of the program lies in quality childcare, not education. By providing a safe, healthy place for children to spend their day it allows economically deprived mothers to find paid employment, thereby improving the quality of the home and economic wellbeing of the family. Consistent with this view are the results of a research study that took advantage of the fact that Head Start centers vary in the services they offer (Walters, 2015). The study revealed more benefits from full-day programs (which would provide mothers the opportunity to work) than from half-day programs and more benefits from programs that included home visits (which would provide the possibility for social services) than from those that did not. In contrast, the education level of the teachers (whether or not they had higher degrees), the kind of educational curriculum used, and the class size had no effect.

We used to talk about programs for young children as daycare or childcare. Those terms have largely gone out of style, and we are now much more likely to talk about them as preschool. My hypothesis is that Head Start and other programs for young children would work better if we removed the schoolishness from them and reverted to a greater focus on care and less on training. Care means attending to the real needs of children and families. For children that means providing them with healthy meals, medical attention, a safe place to spend the day, and lots of opportunity to play and explore with other kids. For families in poverty it means benefits that allow for an improved standard of living at home, which might come in part from paid employment for a parent. If these are provided, academic improvement will follow; it doesn't have to be forced.

References

Bailey, M., Sun, S., & Timpe, B. (2018). *Prep school for kids: The long-run impacts of Head Start on human capital and economic self-sufficiency.* Working paper, downloaded at http://www-personal.umich.edu/~baileymj/Bailey_Sun_Timpe.pdf

Bakken, L., Brown, N., & Downing, B. (2017). Early childhood education: The long-term benefits. *Journal of Research in Childhood Education*, 31, 255-259.

Deming, D. (2009). Early childhood intervention and life-cycle skill development: Evidence from Head Start. *American Economic Journal: Applied Economics*, 1, 111-134.

Fosburg, L. B., et al. (1984). The effects of Head Start health services: Report of the Head Start health evaluation. Report

Prepared for the Administration for Children, Youth and Families, U. S. Department of Health and Human Services. Cambridge, MA: Abt Associates.

Gray, P. (2015a). Early academic training produces long-term harm. Freedom to Learn blog, *Psychology Today*. Downloaded at https://www.psychologytoday.com/us/blog/freedom-learn/201505/
early-academic-training-produces-long-term-harm

Gray, P. (2015b). How early academic training retards intellectual development. . Freedom to Learn blog, *Psychology Today*. Downloaded at https://www.psychologytoday.com/us/blog/
freedom-learn/201506/
how-early-academic-training-retards-intellectual-development

Lipsey, M., Farran, D., & Durkin, K. (2018). Effects of the Tennessee prekindergarten program on children's achievement and behavior through third grade. *Early Childhood Research Quarterly*, 45, 155-176.

Ludwig, J., & Miller, D. (2007). Does Head Start improve childen's life chances? Evidence from a regression discontinuity design. *Quarterly Journal of Economics*, Feb., 2007, 150-208.

Pages, R., Lukes, D., Bailey, D., & Duncan, G. (2019). Elusive longer-run impacts of Head Start: replications within and across cohorts. Working paper, downloaded at https://arxiv.org/pdf/1903.01954.pdf

Piper, K. (2018). Early childhood education yields big benefits—just not the ones you think. *Vox*, Oct. 16, 2018.

Piper, K. (2019). Study: Head start improves kids' lives. But we're still finding out just how. *Vox*, Jan. 8, 2019.

Schanzenbach, D., & Bauer, L. (2016). The long-term impact of the Head Start program. Brookings Report, Aug. 19, 2016.

Straight Talk (2018). Large randomized trial finds state pre-K program has adverse effects on academic achievement. Reform is needed to increase effectiveness. Downloaded at https://

www.straighttalkonevidence.org/2018/07/16/large-randomized
-controlled-trial-finds-state-pre-k-program-has-adverse-
effects-on-academic-achievement/

Walters, C. (2015). Inputs in the production of early childhood
human capital: Evidence from head start. *American Economic
Journal: Applied Economics*, 7, 76-102.

Zigler, E., & Valentine, J. (1979). *Project Head Start: A legacy of the
war on poverty* New York: Free Press.

Sudbury Valley
Framingham

CPSIA information can be obtained
at www.ICGtesting.com
Printed in the USA
BVHW071116010721
610975BV00017B/1019

9 781952 837005